COUNTRY INNS
OF AMERICA
COOKBOOK

Country Inns of America
COOKBOOK

EDITED BY ROBERT R. REID

PHOTOGRAPHS BY
LILO RAYMOND AND GEORGE W. GARDNER

Holt, Rinehart and Winston

NEW YORK

Copyright © 1982 by Knapp Communications Corporation
All rights reserved, including the right to reproduce
this book or portions thereof in any form.
Published by Holt, Rinehart and Winston,
383 Madison Avenue, New York, New York 10017.
Published simultaneously in Canada by Holt, Rinehart
and Winston of Canada, Limited.

Library of Congress Cataloging in Publication Data
Main entry under title:
The country inns of America cookbook.
    Includes index.
    1. Cookery, American.   2. Hotels, taverns, etc.—
United States.   I. Reid, Robert R.
TX715.C8623   641.5   82-6162   AACR2
ISBN 0-03-062174-7

First Edition

Produced and designed by Robert R. Reid with
Tracy Ecclesine, Alan Harvey and George Allen.
Food consultant: Gene Benton
Printed in the United States of America
10 9 8 7 6 5 4 3 2

ISBN 0-03-062174-7

FOREWORD

This book is dedicated to the many innkeepers and chefs whose love of fine food has made this country inns cookbook possible. Because cooking is a great part of an inn's attraction, innkeepers take food very seriously and pride themselves on the way they prepare and serve it.

The book began as a charming, small-scale project, but it has turned into a major accomplishment. Innkeepers' recipes for some of the wonderful dishes they prepare are not in written form. Recipes had to be written down, collected and transcribed. Their terminology and measurements were then edited to standardize regional and stylistic differences. Since much larger quantities are prepared at the inns, quantities also had to be adjusted downward and then re-tested. Afterward, all the edited recipes as they appear in this book were sent back to the inns for their approval.

Except for a few illustrations of soup ingredients, all the photographs—both color and black and white—were taken at the inns. They offer a graphic counterpoint to the descriptions of country inns and their wonderful food. Place settings, as you will see, may be superbly elegant or charmingly simple. Dishes range from sophisticated *haute cuisine* to homey regional fare, all served with inspiring variety. Our grateful thanks go to all the innkeepers and chefs who so generously contributed to this unique cookbook.

CONTENTS

vi

BRUNCH

BUFFET

DINNER

SOUPS

CONTENTS

VEGETABLES

x

BREADS

DESSERTS

BRUNCH

The first meal of the day at many country inns is either a light, continental-style breakfast served on a tray and delivered to the room or a family-style breakfast with one sitting. But on weekends this meal is more elaborate and leisurely and guests arrive, often after a stroll through the environs, to the welcoming aromas of home-baked bread, fresh coffee and entrées sizzling on the grill or warm from the oven. The Egremont Inn, South Egremont, Massachusetts, and the San Ysidro Ranch in Montecito, California, are just two of the inns that offer an extensive brunch.

Bloody Marys, Screwdrivers and Champagne Mimosas are popular drinks at brunch, though some innkeepers offer more original libations. Attractively served fresh fruit or even a cold fruit soup make a pleasant starter to the meal. The ever-popular Eggs Benedict is just one way of presenting eggs. The expert omelet maker, offering a variety of fillings, shines at brunch. It is the emphasis on homemade goods and local produce that makes brunch at a country inn a delight.

2 Baked Grapefruit

CHALET SUZANNE
Lake Wales, Florida

FOR EACH PERSON

½ grapefruit
1 teaspoon (approximate) butter, melted
Sugar
Cinnamon
½ chicken liver
Flour for coating
Salt
Pepper
⅛ teaspoon paprika
Butter or oil for sautéing

Remove center from grapefruit and cut fruit into sections, being careful not to pierce skin. Fill center cavity with melted butter. Sprinkle sugar and cinnamon on top. Place grapefruit under broiler until slightly browned, or in 375°F oven for about 10 minutes.

Roll chicken liver in flour seasoned with salt, pepper and paprika and lightly sauté in butter or oil. Garnish each grapefruit half with sautéed chicken liver.

Granola

FLYING CLOUD INN
New Marlboro, Massachusetts

MAKES 6 POUNDS

1¼ pounds rolled oats
1 pound assorted chopped nuts (cashews, almonds, pecans, etc.)
½ pound unsweetened coconut
½ pound raw wheat germ
½ pound sunflower seeds
½ pound sesame seeds
½ pound roasted unsalted soybeans
½ pound raw unsalted peanuts
⅛ pound bran flakes
¼ cup instant dry milk
¾ cup oil
¾ cup honey
1 teaspoon vanilla
⅓ pound dates
⅓ pound raisins
⅓ pound dried apricots

Preheat oven to 325°F. In large bowl, mix together dry ingredients, including dry milk but not dried fruits. In small saucepan, heat oil, honey and vanilla until well mixed. Add to dry ingredients and mix well. Spread thinly on cookies sheets and bake until a light golden color, about 15 minutes. Turn the mixture frequently.

Cool in large bowls. Add dates, raisins and apricots and store mixture in large glass containers.

Eggs Benedict

COPPER BEECH INN
Ivoryton, Connecticut

6 SERVINGS

3 English muffins
6 slices tomato
2 tablespoons (¼ stick) butter
6 slices Canadian bacon
6 eggs, poached*
Hollandaise Sauce (*see page 176*)
Truffles, sliced (optional)

Split English muffins, toast lightly and keep warm. Sauté tomato slices in 1 tablespoon butter for 1 minute on each side. Sauté bacon slices in remaining butter about 2 minutes on each side. Place muffin halves on serving plates or platter. On each half, place a slice of bacon topped with slice of tomato and a poached egg. Cover eggs with hot Hollandaise Sauce and sprinkle with truffles.

* Eggs may be poached in advance and kept in a bowl of warm water. When ready to serve, remove with a slotted spoon and pat dry with paper towel.

CHALET SUZANNE'S BAKED GRAPEFRUIT

The Baked Grapefruit, like many other creations, originated because of a lucky accident. It made its debut when Carl and Vita Hinshaw, proprietors of the Chalet Suzanne in Lake Wales, Florida, were playing host to a group of food editors. Because the Hinshaws were running behind schedule, they combined two courses by placing chicken livers on top of baked grapefruit. Their creation was an instant hit that has become a much-loved feature of the inn.

Tangy Baked Eggs

SUTTER CREEK INN
Sutter Creek, California

12 SERVINGS*

  6 English muffins, split, toasted and buttered
  1 can condensed cream of celery soup
  1 can condensed cream of mushroom soup
  ½ cup sour cream
  6 tablespoons chopped green onions
  2 tablespoons Worcestershire sauce
  ¼ cup dry sherry
  2 tablespoons Dijon mustard
  4 teaspoons chopped pimiento
  ½ teaspoon liquid hot pepper seasoning
  ½ teaspoon dry basil
  ½ teaspoon dry oregano
  12 extra large eggs
  1 cup grated Parmesan cheese
  ½ teaspoon paprika

Keep muffins in a warm place. In medium bowl, mix soups, sour cream, green onions, Worcestershire sauce, sherry, mustard, pimiento, hot pepper seasoning, basil and oregano. Spread this sauce into two 9 × 13-inch baking pans.

Break eggs onto sauce and sprinkle with cheese and paprika. Bake uncovered in 325°F oven until whites are set, about 25 minutes. Lift each egg out onto muffin half, spoon sauce on top. Serve immediately.

* Recipe may be cut in half to serve 6. Sherry may be adjusted to taste.

Omelet Café Procope

PUMP HOUSE INN
Canadensis, Pennsylvania

FOR EACH PERSON

  ¼ cup Alaskan king crabmeat, rinsed and drained
  1 teaspoon grated blue cheese
  ½ teaspoon fresh lemon juice

  2 tablespoons (¼ stick) butter
  2 teaspoons diced onions
  2 small mushrooms, diced

  2 eggs
    Pinch salt
    Freshly ground black pepper—1 turn of pepper mill
    Small pinch tarragon
    Small pinch chives
  2 tablespoons whipping cream (optional)
  2 tablespoons (¼ stick) butter

Toss crabmeat with lemon juice and blue cheese and set aside.

Heat 10-inch omelet pan over moderate heat for 3 minutes. Melt 2 tablespoons butter and add onions and mushrooms. Cook 3 to 4 minutes, stirring frequently.

Break eggs into large bowl; add salt, pepper, herbs and cream. Beat thoroughly. Stir in onions and mushrooms. Heat remaining butter in pan over medium heat until bubbly.

Pour in omelet mixture. With wooden spoon, push cooked eggs towards center and tilt pan so uncooked egg fills empty spaces. When eggs are almost done but still soft, add crabmeat and cheese. Shake pan back and forth and fold omelet in half. Brown each side.

Herbed Creamy Cheese Omelet

SUTTER CREEK INN
Sutter Creek, California

1 TO 2 SERVINGS

  ½ cup softened cream cheese, ricotta or cottage cheese
  1 tablespoon snipped chives
  1 tablespoon chopped fresh basil
  3 eggs
  2 tablespoons cream
    Salt
    Freshly ground pepper
  1 tablespoon butter

Combine cheese, chives and basil and set aside. Beat eggs, cream, salt and pepper with fork. Heat butter in 10-inch omelet pan. When butter bubbles, pour in egg mixture, which should set at edges at once. Lift edges and underside with fork and tilt pan as necessary so uncooked egg can flow underneath. When top is moist and creamy, spoon cheese mixture on half of omelet. With pancake turner, fold in half or roll, then turn out onto heated platter.

The famous
Baked Grapefruit
from Chalet Suzanne,
Lake Wales, Florida.
See page 2.

4 Spanish Omelet

SUTTER CREEK INN
Sutter Creek, California

6 SERVINGS

- 2 16-ounce cans stewed tomatoes
- 2 teaspoons cornstarch

- 9 eggs
- ¾ cup milk
   Salt
   Pepper
- 3 tablespoons (⅜ stick) butter
- ¾ cup shredded cheddar cheese

   Parmesan cheese, grated
- ¼ cup minced scallions
- ¼ cup minced parsley

Reserve ½ cup liquid from stewed tomatoes. Place remaining contents of cans in 2-quart saucepan and break up tomatoes with spoon. Blend cornstarch with reserved liquid, add to tomatoes, cook and stir until thickened.

Break eggs into large bowl and add milk, salt and pepper to taste and beat until foamy. Heat butter in 12-inch skillet, add egg mixture and cook slowly. Run spatula around edge, lifting to allow uncooked portion to flow underneath. Cover until mixture is almost set. Sprinkle cheddar cheese over omelet and cover until cheese melts. Turn out onto warm platter. Pour stewed tomatoes over top. Sprinkle with Parmesan cheese, scallions and parsley and serve immediately.

Cheese Strata

THE MAINSTAY
Cape May, New Jersey

6 TO 8 SERVINGS

Prepare the night before serving. As a variation, add shrimp or diced ham.

   Butter for greasing dish
- 8 slices firm-textured white bread with crusts, cubed
- 1½ cups grated sharp cheddar cheese
- 8 large eggs
- 2 cups milk
- 4 tablespoons (½ stick) butter, melted
- ½ teaspoon dry mustard

Preheat oven to 350°F. Butter a 2-quart soufflé dish, ceramic or stoneware casserole, or 9 × 5 × 3-inch ovenproof glass loaf dish. Layer dish with bread and cheese, beginning with bread and ending with cheese. Combine eggs, milk, melted butter and mustard in a blender. Blend thoroughly on high speed, about 10 seconds. Pour over bread and cheese and refrigerate overnight. Bake at 350°F until firm in the center when pressed lightly, 45 to 60 minutes.

Fresh Salmon Quiche

1770 HOUSE
East Hampton, New York

4 TO 6 SERVINGS

CRUST
- 1 cup flour
- ½ cup (1 stick) sweet butter
- 4 ounces cream cheese

FILLING
- 3 tablespoons breadcrumbs
- 1½ cups grated Swiss cheese
- ⅓ cup grated Parmesan cheese
- 1½ cups cooked fresh salmon, coarsely flaked

- 3 eggs
- 1½ cups half and half
- 2 tablespoons finely chopped dill
   Dill sprigs for decoration

FOR CRUST: Combine flour, butter and cream cheese in processor or place flour in bowl and cut in butter and cream cheese by hand, and form into ball. Chill dough for 30 minutes. Roll out on floured surface to fit a 9-inch quiche or pie pan. Fit unbaked crust in pan and refrigerate until ready to use. Preheat oven to 375°F.

FOR FILLING: Sprinkle breadcrumbs over unbaked crust. Mix Swiss and Parmesan cheeses and distribute evenly over breadcrumbs. Arrange salmon over cheeses.

Mix eggs and half and half together until well blended and pour over contents in shell. Sprinkle chopped dill over top. Bake in lower third of oven until quiche is set and golden brown, about 35 to 40 minutes. Allow to cool slightly, decorate with dill sprigs and serve.

Eggs Benedict from the Copper Beech Inn, Ivoryton, Connecticut. *See page* 2.

Stuffed Eggs
from Old Drover's Inn, Dover Plains, New York.
See page 22.

Oysters à la Gino from Robert Morris Inn, Oxford, Maryland. *See page 35.*

A Terrine
from Stonehenge,
Ridgefield, Connecticut
See page 25.

OVERLEAF:
Making Crepes Suzettes
at the Elms Inn,
Ridgefield, Connecticut.
For complete description
of the procedures
see pages 18–19.

Oysters à la Gino from Robert Morris Inn, Oxford, Maryland. *See page 35.*

A Terrine
from Stonehenge,
Ridgefield, Connecticut
See page 25.

OVERLEAF:
Making Crepes Suzettes
at the Elms Inn,
Ridgefield, Connecticut.
For complete description
of the procedures
see pages 18–19.

Fresh Salmon Quiche from 1770 House, East Hampton, New York. *See page* 4.

Crepes St. Jacques from the Bramble Inn, Brewster, Massachusetts. *See page* 17.

Quiche Légumes

BLACK BASS HOTEL
Lumberville, Pennsylvania

3 TO 4 SERVINGS

- 1 cup fresh asparagus, cut into ¼-inch pieces
- 1 medium onion, thinly sliced
- 4 medium mushrooms, sliced
- 2–3 tablespoons (¼–⅜ stick) butter, room temperature
- 4 eggs
- 1 cup heavy cream
- 1 cup milk
- ½ teaspoon salt
- ⅛ teaspoon white pepper or to taste
- ⅛ teaspoon nutmeg or to taste
  9-inch pie crust, baked
  (*see page 176*)

Preheat oven to 350°F. In medium skillet, sauté asparagus, onion and mushrooms in butter over moderate heat for 5 minutes. Onions should be quite soft and lightly colored. Beat eggs, cream, milk, salt, pepper and nutmeg thoroughly, add sautéed vegetables. Slowly pour quiche mixture into baked pie crust and bake until custard is firm in the center, about 20 minutes.

Spinach and Onion Quiche

WHEATLEIGH
Lenox, Massachusetts

6 SERVINGS

CRUST
- 1 cup all purpose flour
- ¼ teaspoon salt
- 6 tablespoons (¾ stick) butter, room temperature
- 1 egg yolk
- 1 tablespoon cold water

FILLING
- ½–¾ pound spinach, chopped, or 10-ounce package frozen spinach, defrosted and squeezed dry
- 1 small onion, chopped and sautéed until limp
- ½ cup heavy cream
- ½ cup milk
- 4 eggs, slightly beaten
  Dash cayenne
  Dash salt
  Generous dash nutmeg
- 6 ounces Gruyère cheese, coarsely grated

FOR CRUST: Sift flour and salt into mixing bowl. Add butter and blend lightly with fingertips or pastry blender until mixture resembles breadcrumbs. In separate bowl, beat egg yolk while slowly adding water. Sprinkle yolk mixture over dough and work in lightly with hands. Press dough into ball, wrap in foil and refrigerate at least 1 hour. Preheat oven to 450°F. Roll dough between two sheets of waxed paper, forming a circle ⅛ inch thick and 1 inch larger than 9- or 10-inch quiche or pie pan. Line pan with dough. Cover dough with aluminum foil weighed down with beans or rice. Bake until crust is set, about 10 to 15 minutes. While crust is baking, prepare custard filling.

FOR FILLING: If using fresh spinach, place just enough water in 1½-quart saucepan to cover bottom of pan, and bring to boil over high flame. Add spinach and cover tightly. Cook until spinach is just wilted, 3 to 5 minutes. Drain thoroughly in colander and press out any remaining water. Cool spinach. In large bowl, mix onion and cooled or defrosted spinach together. Use blender to combine cream, milk, eggs, cayenne, salt and nutmeg. Pour about ½ to 1 cup mixture into onion and spinach. Mix well with spoon.

TO ASSEMBLE: Lower oven temperature to 350°F. Remove foil and weights from baked crust and cover crust with two-thirds of onion and spinach mixture. Cover with Gruyère. Pour in remainder of liquid. Top with remaining onion and spinach. Bake until filling is puffed and golden and resists light finger pressure in center, about 30 to 40 minutes. Serve warm.

14 Crabcakes

Crab Crown Pompadour

RED FOX TAVERN
Middleburg, Virginia

4 SERVINGS

- 2 eggs
- 1 pound backfin or lump crabmeat (Dungeness crab may be substituted)
- 1 cup fresh breadcrumbs
- ⅔ cup (scant) mayonnaise
- 4 rounded tablespoons minced onion
- 2 rounded tablespoons minced celery
- 1 tablespoon lemon juice
- 1 tablespoon Worcestershire sauce
- 2 teaspoons Old Bay seasoning (or substitute ¼ teaspoon each celery salt and white pepper, ⅛ teaspoon each dry mustard, ground bay leaf, ground cardamom, mace, ginger, ground cassia bark and paprika)
  Salt and pepper to taste
  Pinch minced garlic (optional)
  Few drops hot pepper sauce (optional)
- ¼ cup oil for frying

In large mixing bowl, beat eggs, flake in crabmeat, add remaining ingredients except oil and mix all together thoroughly. Form into 8 patties. Heat oil in large skillet and fry patties on each side until golden brown, adding more oil to pan if necessary.

INN FOR ALL SEASONS
Scituate Harbor, Massachusetts

2 SERVINGS

- ½ cup (1 stick) butter
- 6–8 slices firm white bread, crusts trimmed
- 1 egg
- 2 cups half and half
- 1 teaspoon snipped fresh chives
  Salt and freshly ground pepper to taste
- 6 ounces crab leg meat
  Pompadour Sauce*

Line two small or one 12-ounce porcelain ramekin with parchment paper. In 6-inch skillet or small shallow pan, melt butter. Dip bread into melted butter and fit into ramekin, overlapping slices. Trim bread where necessary. Refrigerate to set.

Preheat oven to 400°F. In mixing bowl, blend egg, half and half, chives, salt and pepper. Arrange crabmeat in bread-lined ramekin. Pour egg and half and half mixture over crabmeat. Place ramekin in shallow pan of hot water and bake until custard is set, about 45 minutes. Invert ramekin on serving plate and remove parchment paper. Serve covered with Pompadour Sauce.

*Pompadour Sauce

MAKES ABOUT 1 CUP

- 2 tablespoons diced onion
- 2 medium tomatoes, peeled and diced
- 2 tablespoons (¼ stick) butter
- ¼ cup dry white wine
- ½ pound shrimp shells
- 2 celery stalks, chopped
- 1 medium onion, sliced
- 1 cup chicken stock
- 1 bay leaf
- 2 tablespoons half and half
  Salt and freshly ground pepper
- 1 teaspoon chopped truffles (optional)

In 3-inch skillet or 2-cup saucepan, sauté diced onion and tomatoes in 1 tablespoon butter for about 10 minutes to make tomato concasse (rough-textured sauce). Add wine and cook over low heat until reduced by half. Set aside. Melt remaining butter in 8-inch sauté pan. Add shrimp shells, celery and onion and cook until onions are translucent, about 5 minutes. Add chicken stock and bay leaf. Cook over low heat until reduced one half. Strain. Add 2 tablespoons each tomato concasse and half and half, blending gently. Season with salt and pepper and, if desired, garnish with chopped truffles. (Remaining concasse may be reserved for future use in soups, stews or sauces.)

MIRIAM PERLE

From Cooking School to Country Inn

"The Cuisine of Today" is the way Miriam Perle, co-owner of New York's 1770 House describes her inn's food, an eclectic mixture of tastes and styles from many parts of the world. Miriam, a Cordon Bleu graduate, ran a cooking school before she and husband Sid transformed a run-down Long Island boarding house into a top-notch country inn. Today the 1770 House stands proudly in a row of restored colonial homes on East Hampton's main street. Food is Miriam's great love and she still manages to squeeze in a cooking course or two along with her busy career as chef at this charming inn.

Buckwheat Pancakes

MARSHLANDS INN
Sackville, New Brunswick, Canada

MAKES 12 MEDIUM PANCAKES

Prepare the night before serving.

- 2 cups buttermilk
- 1 cup stoneground buckwheat flour
- ⅜ cup all purpose flour
- ½ teaspoon salt
  Oil for cooking
- 2 teaspoons baking soda
- 4 tablespoons warm water
  Maple syrup

Blend together buttermilk, flours and salt and let stand overnight.

Preheat pan to high heat or electric fry pan to 375°–400° F. Cover surface lightly with oil. Dissolve baking soda in warm water and mix with batter. If too thick, dilute with more buttermilk. Batter should pour readily. Ladle batter into the hot pan. Cook pancakes until bubbles appear on surface and begin to burst and edges are golden brown, about 3 minutes. Turn and cook until other side is brown, about 2 minutes. Serve with pure maple syrup.

Fresh Corn Cakes

SUTTER CREEK INN
Sutter Creek, California

MAKES 35 TO 40 PANCAKES

- 8 ears fresh corn
- 4 cups flour
- ¼ cup sugar
- 4 teaspoons baking powder
- 3 teaspoons salt
- ½ teaspoon pepper
- 6 eggs
- 1½ cups (or more) milk
- ¼ cup (½ stick) butter, melted
  Oil for cooking
  Butter, room temperature

Cut corn from cobs. In large bowl, combine flour, sugar, baking powder, salt and pepper. In separate large bowl, beat eggs until thick and lemon colored; stir in milk and melted butter until well mixed. Blend into flour mixture until well moistened. Stir in corn. If batter is too thick, add more milk (it should pour thickly but easily). Lightly coat griddle or large frying pan with oil and heat. Griddle is ready when a few drops of water spattered on griddle sizzle. Drop batter by the tablespoon onto hot griddle. Fry cakes until they bubble, then brown around edges, about 3 minutes. Turn and cook until other side is brown, about 3 minutes. Serve with butter.

Berkshire Apple Pancake

RED LION INN
Stockbridge, Massachusetts

2 SERVINGS

- 2 medium tart apples (about 3½ cups)
- 2 cups flour
- 3 tablespoons sugar
- 1 tablespoon baking powder
- ½ teaspoon salt
- ½ teaspoon cinnamon
- 1⅓ cups milk
- ½ teaspoon vanilla
- 3 tablespoons (⅜ stick) butter
  Brown sugar and maple syrup

Preheat oven to 450°F. Peel, core and thinly slice apples. In mixing bowl, combine flour, sugar, baking powder, salt, cinnamon, then milk and vanilla, mixing until smooth. Melt butter in 12-inch ovenproof skillet. Cover bottom of pan with apples and cover them with batter. Bake until bottom is golden brown, about 10 to 15 minutes. Turn by flipping pancake over onto plate then sliding it back into pan, apple side up. Continue baking until other side is golden brown, about 10 to 15 minutes. Remove from pan, sprinkle with brown sugar and serve with maple syrup.

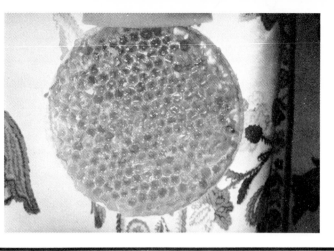

"We are fortunate to have a source of honey nearby," says the head cook at the Flying Cloud Inn in New Marlboro, Massachusetts. "A member of our staff has his own beehives, which supply us with wonderful Goldenrod and Wildflower honey. Homegrown produce is essential to all our cooking," she adds, "and we use

16 Raised Dough Waffles

INN AT STARLIGHT LAKE
Starlight, Pennsylvania

MAKES 4 TO 6 WAFFLES

Batter must be allowed to rise at least 8 hours or overnight.

  2 tablespoons dry yeast
2½ cups warm water (105–115°F)
  ½ cup dry milk
  ½ cup salad oil
  1 teaspoon salt
  1 teaspoon sugar
1½ cups white flour
  ½ cup whole wheat flour
  ¼ cup wheat germ
  2 eggs, well beaten
    Pinch baking soda
    Butter, room temperature
    Syrup

In large mixing bowl, dissolve yeast in ½ cup water. Let stand 5 minutes. Stir in remaining water, dry milk, salad oil, salt and sugar. Separately add white flour, whole wheat flour and wheat germ, beating after each addition. Mix well. Cover bowl with a tea towel and let stand overnight in warm place. Bowl should be large enough to allow batter to triple in size. In morning, add eggs and baking soda. Mix well. Pour about ⅓ cup of batter into heated waffle iron. Bake until golden brown, about 5 to 7 minutes. Serve at once with butter and syrup.

Crepe Batter

ELMS INN
Ridgefield, Connecticut

MAKES 20 TO 30 CREPES

  4 eggs
1½ cups flour
    Pinch salt
1½ cups milk
    Melted butter (as needed)

In medium bowl, combine eggs, flour and salt and gradually whisk in milk to make a smooth batter. Allow to stand until mixture is thick enough to thinly coat spoon. Heat 6-inch heavy skillet or crepe pan until very hot, brush with butter and pour in just enough batter to thinly cover bottom of pan. Tilt pan to spread batter, and pour off excess. Return to heat. Cook until top glazes and crepe shakes loose from bottom of pan, about 1 to 2 minutes. Turn with spatula or flip over and lightly brown other side. Turn out onto linen kitchen towel and repeat process for rest of batter. Set aside on warm plate until ready to fill. May be frozen or refrigerated between pieces of waxed paper for later use.

Crepes St. Jacques

BRAMBLE INN
Brewster, Massachusetts

MAKES 10 CREPES

CREPES
  2 eggs
  2 egg yolks
  ⅛ teaspoon salt
  1 cup flour
  ½ cup milk
  ½ cup water
  1 tablespoon butter, melted
    Melted butter (as needed)

FILLING
  1 cup sliced fresh mushrooms
1½ tablespoons finely chopped onion
  ¼ pound scallops, chopped
  ¼ pound scrod
  ⅓ cup dry white wine
  3 tablespoons (⅜ stick) butter
  3 tablespoons flour
  ½ teaspoon salt
1½ cups half and half
  2 tablespoons clam broth
  2 tablespoons chopped fresh parsley
    Parsley sprigs (garnish)

FOR CREPES: In large mixing bowl, combine eggs, egg yolks and salt. Gradually add flour alternately with milk and water, beating until smooth. Beat in 1 tablespoon melted butter. Refrigerate batter at least 1 hour. When ready to make crepes, stir batter until smooth. Heat 8-inch heavy skillet or crepe pan very hot, brush with melted butter and pour in just enough batter to lightly cover bottom. Tilt pan to spread batter, honey in our homemade cereals and, of course, in all our baking." The Flying Cloud's recipe for Granola may be found in this book.

Those who know only bland supermarket honey should seek out the many other varieties including Tupelo, Orange Blossom, Sourwood and Piedmont.

Strawberry Crepes

THE MAINSTAY
Cape May, New Jersey

6 TO 8 SERVINGS

CREPES

1¼ cups milk
¾ cup flour
1 egg
1 egg yolk
1 tablespoon butter, melted
Melted butter (as needed)
Pinch salt
2 pints fresh strawberries, hulled
Sugar to taste
6–8 ¼-inch pats butter, room temperature

SAUCE

1 pound package frozen strawberries, defrosted
¼ cup sugar
1 tablespoon cornstarch

FOR CREPES: In blender, combine milk, flour, egg, egg yolk, melted butter and salt; blend well. Heat 6-inch iron or heavy aluminum skillet very hot, brush with butter and pour in just enough batter to lightly cover bottom. Tilt pan to spread batter, and pour off excess. Return to heat. Cook until top glazes and crepe shakes loose from pan, about 1 to 2 minutes. Turn with spatula and very lightly brown other side. Repeat until all crepes are done. Stack between pieces of waxed paper and set aside. Crepes may be stored in refrigerator overnight.

When ready to serve, preheat oven to 300°F. Grease shallow baking pan; set aside. Halve 15 of the larg-

and pour off excess. Return to heat. Cook until top glazes and crepe shakes loose from bottom of pan, about 1 to 2 minutes. Turn with spatula or flip over and lightly brown other side. Turn out onto linen towel and repeat process for rest of batter. Set aside on warm plate until ready to use.

FOR FILLING: In 8-inch skillet, simmer mushrooms, onion, scallops and scrod in wine until scrod flakes, about 5 minutes; set aside. In 12-inch skillet over low heat, melt butter, stir in flour and salt and cook, stirring constantly, for 2 minutes. Add half and half and stir until thickened. Add clam broth, fish mixture and chopped parsley. Place about ¼ to ⅓ cup in center of each crepe and roll up. Serve hot, garnished with sprig of parsley.

est, best berries. Sprinkle with sugar; set aside. Slice remaining berries and sprinkle with sugar to taste. Place about 2 tablespoons on each crepe and roll up. Place in baking pan, dot with butter pats and warm in oven for 5 minutes. Do not overheat or berries will become too soft. To serve, place two warmed crepes on each plate. Top with reserved halved berries and pour warmed strawberry sauce over all. Any remaining sauce may be reserved for future use as ice cream topping.

FOR SAUCE: Puree strawberries in blender. Add sugar and cornstarch, blend or stir until dissolved. Pour into 1-quart saucepan, bring to low boil and cook over medium heat until thickened and slightly darkened, about 3 to 4 minutes. Stir well and keep warm.

MAKING CREPES SUZETTE

Using the basic Crepe Batter, Heinz Huegen, Maitre d'Hotel of the Elms Inn in Ridgefield, Connecticut, demonstrates the process for making Crepes Suzette. The rind of one orange is grated into the crepes suzette pan; The juice of the orange and of one lemon are squeezed over the rind.

The pan is placed over medium heat.

Two tablespoons (¼ stick) of butter are added. Two teaspoons of sugar are sprinkled over the mixture.

The sauce is heated until the sugar begins to caramelize.

Six crepes are folded and placed in the pan. An ounce of Cointreau is poured in slowly, covering each crepe.

The crepes are turned and an ounce of Grand Marnier is poured over the crepes.

The sauce is brought to a boil, then an ounce of good brandy is poured into it. The alcohol is burned off just before serving.

Another way to celebrate breakfast is at the Black Bass Hotel in Lumberville, Pennsylvania, overlooking the sleepy Delaware River. More than two centuries of travelers have feasted on this early morning sight after slumbering in an inn as tranquil as the river below.

20 Fried Apples

THE MAINSTAY
Cape May, New Jersey

6 SERVINGS

8–10 medium red apples (Red Delicious preferred)
  6 strips lean bacon
  ½ cup firmly packed brown sugar

Core apples and peel in vertical strips to make alternate red and white stripes. Slice thinly. Rinse in colander (to remove bits of loose skin) and set aside. Cook bacon in Dutch oven over medium heat until crisp. Remove and drain on paper towels. Pour off fat from Dutch oven. Add apples and top with brown sugar. Cover and cook over low to medium heat until apples are thoroughly steamed, about 20 to 25 minutes. Crumble bacon and cook with apples for last 2 to 3 minutes. Serve warm.

Lemon Butter

CHALET SUZANNE
Lake Wales, Florida

MAKES ABOUT 1 CUP

  ½ cup sugar
  2 eggs
  2 tablespoons flour
    Juice of 2 lemons
    Pinch salt

In double boiler over boiling water, combine all ingredients. Mix well and cook until thick, stirring constantly. Cool and serve as spread for toast, rolls or muffins.

Esther's Jam

JAMES HOUSE
Port Townsend, Washington

MAKES ABOUT 12 PINTS

  3 pounds fresh ripe unpeeled apricots, pitted and thinly sliced
2½–3 boxes fresh raspberries
 30 ounces canned crushed pineapple, drained
    Sugar

Put fruit in large bowl and weigh it, then empty fruit into a 6- to 8-quart heavy-bottomed saucepan. If aluminum is used, make sure inside is bright to prevent darkening of fruit. In same bowl used to weigh fruit, add sugar to equal weight of fruit. Add this to saucepan, stir thoroughly, then bring to a steady rolling boil on medium to high heat, stirring constantly to prevent scorching or sticking. Reduce heat to maintain a low boil. Cook, stirring often, until thick enough for a teaspoonful to retain its shape when dropped on a plate to cool, about 20 minutes. Seal in sterilized jars while hot.

Three Fruits Marmalade

MARSHLANDS INN
Sackville, New Brunswick, Canada

MAKES 5 CUPS

Prepare at least a day before serving.

  ½ large grapefruit
  ½ large orange
  ½ lemon
  5 cups cold water
  5 cups sugar

Quarter unpeeled fruit and slice paper thin. Place slices in 3-quart preserving kettle or heavy saucepan with cold water. Let stand overnight.

Boil until fruit is tender and liquid has thickened, at least 4 hours. Add sugar and stir until sugar is dissolved. Continue to boil until mixture reaches 222°F on a candy thermometer. (This temperature is crucial and must be reached although it may take 45 minutes to rise from 200°F to 222°F.) Pour hot marmalade into sterilized ½-pint jars and seal.

BUFFET

Buffet meals may be impressively grand or pleasingly informal; either way, a buffet is the perfect solution to serving a large number of guests and is very popular at country inns. Local residents as well as guests enjoy the daily luncheon buffet served by the Old Mill Inn in Bernardsville, New Jersey, and a Saturday night buffet is a feature of the Heritage House, Little River, California. The number and variety of dishes set forth are limited only by the chef's ambition and the available serving pieces. Nothing is more inviting than a handsomely appointed buffet laden with an array of tempting food—bowls of colorful salads, platters of garnishes, hot dishes simmering in chafing dishes or over other simple warming devices. Almost any food served at a sit-down dinner is suitable, but certain culinary specialties are ideal for a buffet, and several are suggested here.

THE CHANTICLEER INN

Taking an annual food holiday at Nantucket's Chanticleer Inn is an event many out-of-towners look forward to all year long. For locals in the sleepy town of Siasconset, Massachusetts, Chanticleer is *the* place to dine, for the cuisine is always first rate. The man tasting the sauces in the kitchen or smoking eels out back is the inn's French owner, Jean Charles Berruet, who was practically given the inn by former owners to entice him to stay on in the kitchen.

22 Stuffed Eggs with Hickory-Smoked Salt

OLD DROVER'S INN
Dover Plains, New York

6 TO 8 SERVINGS

- 12 hard-cooked eggs, peeled and halved lengthwise
- ⅓ cup mayonnaise
- 1 tablespoon white vinegar
- ½ teaspoon dry mustard
- ¼ teaspoon curry powder
- 3 teaspoons hickory-smoked salt or to taste

Scoop egg yolks into medium bowl and mash with fork. Add mayonnaise, vinegar, mustard and curry powder and blend well. Spoon into pastry bag fitted with fluted or star tip. Pipe into reserved egg whites. Refrigerate for at least two hours. Just before serving, lightly sprinkle the eggs with hickory-smoked salt.

Pâté de Lapin (Rabbit Pâté)

CHANTICLEER INN
Siasconset, Massachusetts

8 SERVINGS

Prepare 2 days in advance.

- ½ pound boneless pork butt, half fat and half lean (if too lean, add ¼ pound fat back)
- ½ pound rabbit, boned and trimmed of skin and gristle
- ¼ cup (approximate) Cognac
  Salt and pepper
- ½ pound chicken livers
- 1 tablespoon butter
- ½ pound boneless veal, trimmed of fat and gristle
- 4 shallots, minced
- 1 garlic clove, minced
- 4 egg yolks
- 1 cup heavy cream
  Pinch each: cloves, nutmeg, ginger and cayenne pepper or to taste
- ¼ cup raisins
- 1½ teaspoons whole juniper berries

  Thin strips of fresh fat back, ⅛ inch thick, to line mold
- 1 10¾-ounce can chicken consommé, condensed or diluted
- 1 envelope unflavored gelatin
- 2 tablespoons cold water or consommé
- 1 10-ounce jar cornichons (garnish)

Cut a dozen long thin strips from pork and rabbit to use inside pâté. Put in small bowl and add Cognac and salt and pepper to taste; marinate overnight in refrigerator.

Preheat oven to 325°F. In 8-inch skillet, sauté chicken livers in butter over moderate heat until evenly browned, about 3 to 4 minutes. Cool and set aside. In grinder using medium blade or in processor with chopping blade, grind together remaining pork, rabbit, veal, chicken livers, shallots and garlic, adding fat back if pork is too lean. Mixture should be a bit coarse. In large bowl, combine meat with egg yolks, cream, Cognac from marinade, salt and pepper and spices. Mix well and stir in raisins and juniper berries.

Line bottom and sides of 9 × 5-inch 2-quart pyrex loaf dish with strips of fat back. Cover tightly with heavy foil. Set loaf dish in pan filled with enough warm water to come about two-thirds of way up sides of loaf dish. Bake until pâté has pulled away from sides of dish, about 1½ hours. Remove from oven and water pan. Uncover and spoon about two-thirds melted fat off top and discard. In small saucepan, bring consommé to boil. Soften gelatin in cold water. In 2-cup measuring cup, pour boiling consommé over gelatin and stir until completely dissolved. Slowly pour 1 cup gelatin mixture over pâté until absorbed. Recover top of pâté with foil. Cover foil with 3-pound board that fits inside top of loaf dish, or fit bottom of another loaf dish with 3-pound weight inside, to compress pâté. Let cool to room temperature. Refrigerate overnight, weighted down. Remove weights and foil and invert onto platter. Serve chilled in slices garnished with cornichons.

Every great chef has a favorite pâté recipe. Pâtés and terrines fit well into the busy schedule of a country inn chef in that they can be made well in advance and chilled until serving time. The skill lies in blending the flavors and creating an appetizing appearance.

At the Pilgrim's Inn, Deer Isle, Maine, innkeeper Eleanor Pavloff serves pâté in the common room before dinner so guests can get to know each other. The pâté recipes

24 Pâté de Coquilles St. Jacques (Scallop Pâté)

CHANTICLEER INN
Siasconset, Massachusetts

8 TO 10 SERVINGS

Prepare 1 day in advance.

PÂTÉ

- ¼ pound bay scallops or very small sea scallops (at least 12)
- ½ pound fillet of sole or bass or combination of both
  Large bunch parsley, chopped
- ⅓ cup (approximate) white wine
- ¼ pound spinach leaves, stems removed
- 1 small bunch watercress, stems removed
- ½ pound sorrel leaves, stems removed
- 2 pounds Canadian sea scallops
- 1 large or 2 small garlic cloves
- 3 egg whites
  Salt and pepper to taste
- 1 tablespoon chopped fresh tarragon
- 1 egg yolk
- 2 tablespoons olive oil
- 1 pound mushrooms, minced
- 2 shallots, minced
  Butter

SAUCE

- 1 pound tomatoes, peeled and seeded
- 2 cups ricotta cheese
- 1 cup yogurt
- ½ cup heavy cream
  Juice of 1 lemon
- 2 tablespoons Armagnac or Cognac
- 2 teaspoons catsup
  Few drops hot pepper sauce
  Salt and pepper
- 1 tablespoon chopped parsley
- ½ tablespoon chopped tarragon

FOR PÂTÉ: In medium bowl, place bay or small sea scallops. Add fish fillets cut into long narrow strips. Add parsley and enough wine to cover seafood. Refrigerate for 2 hours. Into 2-quart pan of boiling water, drop together spinach, watercress and sorrel to blanch. Allow water to come back to full boil. Drain. Run cold water over greens to cool rapidly. Drain. Cover with ice cubes; set aside.

Preheat oven to 400°F. In processor with steel blade or in blender, in batches combine Canadian sea scallops and garlic; process finely. Add egg whites, salt and pepper. Process again. Press all water out of blanched greens. Add to scallop and egg white mixture. Add tarragon and process thoroughly. Add egg yolk and process again until mixture is blended very fine and is light and fluffy. In 10-inch skillet, heat olive oil and add mushrooms and shallots. Lightly sprinkle with salt and sauté over medium heat until mushrooms are lightly browned and rid of excess moisture, about 7 to 10 minutes.

Generously butter 9 × 5-inch 2-quart pyrex loaf pan. Line bottom with half of processed scallop mixture. Layer with half of mushrooms. Remove most parsley from marinated seafood and discard. Place marinated scallops lengthwise along center of mushroom layer. Place marinated fish strips lengthwise on mushrooms to form long ribbons on either side of scallops. Layer remaining mushrooms over all. Cover with remaining processed scallop mixture and smooth with spatula. Cover tightly with foil. Place loaf pan in 9 × 13-inch baking pan. Fill with enough warm water to reach two-thirds of way up sides of loaf pan. Bake until pâté is firm and completely opaque, about 50 minutes. Remove from oven and cool to room temperature. Refrigerate overnight. Serve very cold in slices with sauce.

FOR SAUCE: Cut tomatoes into ⅛-inch dice and place in strainer to drain; set aside. In blender, puree ricotta, yogurt and cream. Add lemon juice, Armagnac or Cognac, catsup, hot pepper sauce and salt and pepper to taste and blend thoroughly. Pour sauce into serving bowl. Stir in parsley, tarragon and well-drained tomatoes.

Tomatoes may be blended with cheese mixture but Chef Berruet believes sauce is better as given in recipe. According to M. Berruet, the blend of ricotta, yogurt and cream closely resembles *fromage blanc*, which is unavailable in this country, much to his regret.

included here show how varied the ingredients can be, from the Rabbit Pâté to the Pâté de Coquilles St. Jacques, both specialties of the Chanticleer. Stonehenge in Ridgefield, Connecticut, serves a terrine that combines pork, veal and chicken livers with pistachios.

As part of a buffet or as an hors d'oeuvre, a homemade pâté is always well received.

Terrine

STONEHENGE
Ridgefield, Connecticut

8 SERVINGS

Prepare 1 day in advance.

- 1 tablespoon butter
- ½ onion, coarsely chopped
- 4 mushroom caps, coarsely chopped
- ½ pound boneless pork, neck and shoulder
- ½ pound boneless stewing veal
- 6 ounces chicken livers
- 2 tablespoons cream
- 2 tablespoons brandy
- 1 teaspoon salt
- 1 teaspoon pepper
- 1 teaspoon allspice
- 2 ounces natural pistachios, shelled and peeled
  Aspic jelly, chicken or veal (optional)

Preheat oven to 300°F. In 6-inch skillet, melt butter and sauté onion and mushrooms until onion is transparent. Allow to cool. Pass pork and veal through grinder, using medium blade. Using fine blade, pass chicken livers through grinder. In small bowl, mix onion and mushrooms with cream, brandy, salt, pepper and allspice. Pass mixture through grinder using fine blade. Add pistachios to ingredients and mix well. Spoon into 1½-quart terrine or 8½ × 4½ × 2½-inch loaf pan. Place terrine in shallow baking pan filled three-quarters full with warm water. Bake terrine uncovered until clear juices show on top or meat mixture starts to come away from sides of terrine, about 1½ hours.

Remove from oven. Cover top with foil. Place 3- to 4-pound weight on top of foil. Cool to room temperature. Remove weight and foil. Drain off excess liquids. Refrigerate for at least 10 hours. If desired, cover with aspic jelly and refrigerate overnight. Turn out onto cutting board to serve.

If using processor instead of grinder, use steel blade. Feed pork and veal through tube and chop to medium consistency using on-off method. Do not puree. Add livers to chopped pork and veal. Place onions, mushrooms, cream, brandy, salt, pepper and allspice in processor bowl. Process to minced consistency. Combine with meat mixture. Add pistachios and mix well.

ST. ORRES
Gualala, California

12 SERVINGS

- 1 pound cream cheese
- 1 pound feta cheese
- ½ pound kasseri cheese, grated
- 1 bunch scallions, chopped
- 1 pound phyllo pastry sheets
- 1 pound (4 sticks) unsalted butter, melted

In large bowl, combine cheeses and scallions. Mix thoroughly with large spoon or mix with hands to break up cheeses. Cut standard sheets of phyllo into 4 strips about 3 inches wide. Keep unused strips covered with waxed paper and a damp cloth while working or they will become brittle. Working 1 strip at a time, lightly butter 4 strips and place one on top of the other to make a layered 4-ply strip. Fold lower right corner of phyllo to left side so that bottom of dough meets left side. Mound 2 teaspoons cheese mixture near bottom left end of strip about 1½ inches from short edge. Fold bottom left corner over filling to form triangle. Working from left to right, fold triangle again and again until whole strip is folded into triangle. Lightly brush top with melted butter. Set aside and cover with plastic wrap and damp cloth. Repeat process until all strips and cheese mixture are used.

Preheat oven to 425°F. Place triangles on ungreased cookie sheet and bake until golden brown, about 10 to 15 minutes. Serve hot.

26 Ginger Wine Cheese Spread

PILGRIM'S INN
Deer Isle, Maine

8 TO 10 SERVINGS

Excellent served with warm wedges of toasted pita bread or with plain crackers. A very good English ginger wine is available at better wine and liquor stores.

½ pound extra sharp white cheddar cheese
Ginger wine
Dash of ground red pepper (optional)

Into medium bowl, grate cheese finely, or cut cheese in chunks and place in processor. Using steel knife, process cheese, turning machine on and off until finely grated. Turn cheese into medium bowl. Add wine gradually, mixing with cheese to make smooth spread. If desired, add red pepper to taste.

Roquefort Mousse Dean

CHALET SUZANNE
Lake Wales, Florida

8 TO 10 SERVINGS

An easy-to-prepare buffet dish, delicious as an hors d'oeuvre, party spread or rich, tangy accompaniment to cooked green vegetables or crudités. May be prepared 2 to 3 days ahead and refrigerated, covered with plastic wrap, in mold.

1½ tablespoons gelatin
4 tablespoons cold water
6 egg yolks
6 tablespoons whipping cream

¾ pound Roquefort or blue cheese
1½ cups whipping cream, whipped
3 egg whites, stiffly beaten
2 tablespoons poppy seeds
Endive or watercress (garnish)

In heatproof cup or small metal bowl, soften gelatin in cold water. Place cup over, or in, hot water and dissolve gelatin; set aside. In 2-quart saucepan, combine egg yolks and cream. Over low heat, without boiling, blend continuously with wire whisk for few minutes until mixture is consistency of thick heavy cream. Stir dissolved gelatin into mixture.

Force Roquefort or blue cheese through fine sieve or process in blender without liquefying. Stir into warm gelatin mixture until smooth. Let cool to room temperature. Fold in cream, egg whites and poppy seeds. Pour into oiled 2-quart mold and chill at least 2 hours. Unmold mousse onto platter and garnish.

Serve with toast rounds or crackers. For a more piquant version, accompany with coarse cracked black pepper and hot pepper sauce or canned slices of chili peppers.

Cheese Hélène

INN FOR ALL SEASONS
Scituate Harbor, Massachusetts

FOR EACH SERVING

2 teaspoons flour
1 large egg, beaten
½ cup breadcrumbs
2 2-inch cubes Gruyère cheese
Oil for deep frying
1 bunch fresh parsley, washed and thoroughly dried
Salt

Place flour, egg and breadcrumbs in separate small bowls. Dip cheese cubes in flour, then egg, then breadcrumbs to coat well. Refrigerate uncovered for about 1 hour. In skillet or deep fryer, heat oil to 400°F. Fry cheese cubes until golden brown and crusty on outside and soft inside, about 2 to 3 minutes. Remove with skimmer or slotted spoon and drain on paper towel. Deep-fry parsley for about 1 minute. Remove and drain on paper towel. Salt to taste.

Arrange parsley on plate and top with fried cheese cubes. Serve with French bread.

ST. ORRES INN

St. Orres in Gualala, California is a country inn that is made largely with recycled materials. The copper sheathing of its handsome domes formerly clad computer equipment. Napkin rings are actually plumber's pipe fittings. The interior walls are lined with a striking arrangement of tongue and groove redwood, carefully put into place by the two master craftsmen who refurbished the inn. St. Orres' three-story dining room is most impressive but the continental cuisine makes an even more memorable statement.

Beer Batter for Chicken, Vegetables or Fruit

PUMP HOUSE INN
Canadensis, Pennsylvania

MAKES ABOUT 2½ CUPS

    1 cup flour
    ½ teaspoon paprika
    ¼ teaspoon baking powder
      Pinch salt
    1 12-ounce bottle beer
      Oil for frying

Heat deep fat fryer to 350°F to 375°F and maintain this temperature throughout cooking time. In medium bowl, combine flour, paprika, baking powder and salt. Add beer and gradually blend until frothy.

FOR CHICKEN: Coat several strips of chicken breast with flour, dip in batter and fry until golden brown, about 8 minutes. Serve with tartar sauce or Chinese duck sauce.

FOR VEGETABLES: Use eggplant strips, zucchini strips, broccoli or cauliflower florets. Coat with flour, dip in batter and cook about 2 to 5 minutes, depending on size. Taste one for doneness.

FOR FRESH FRUIT: Use bananas, cut in half lengthwise, or pears, apples or peaches, sliced into thick rounds. Dip in batter and cook for about 2 to 4 minutes, depending on size. (Cook ripe bananas 2 minutes and green bananas 4 minutes.) Fruits can be served with hot chocolate sauce, vanilla pudding or sugar.

Note: For dessert, any of the following may be added to the beer batter: 1½ teaspoons vanilla extract, ¾ teaspoon almond extract or 1 tablespoon Grand Marnier, rum or other liqueur.

Mussels Vin Blanc

INN FOR ALL SEASONS
Scituate Harbor, Massachusetts

FOR EACH SERVING

    12 mussels, scrubbed and rinsed,
       beards removed
     2 cups water
     2 stalks celery
     1 medium onion
     1 bay leaf
     4 peppercorns
     ⅛ teaspoon salt
       Vin Blanc Sauce*

Tie mussels in a cheesecloth bag. In 4-quart saucepan, combine water, celery, onion, spices and salt. Cover and bring to boil. Lower mussels into liquid, cover and steam until shells open, about 5 minutes. Discard any mussels which do not open. Transfer mussels to large warm glass bowl, and top with Vin Blanc Sauce.

*Vin Blanc Sauce

MAKES ABOUT 2 CUPS

    2 tablespoons (¼ stick) butter
    2 celery stalks, chopped
    1 medium onion, chopped
    1 cup clam juice
    ½ cup white wine (Chardonnay or
      white Burgundy)
    1 bay leaf
      Salt and freshly ground pepper
    1 cup (approximately) half and half

In 1-quart saucepan, melt butter and sauté celery and onion over medium heat until vegetables are translucent, about 5 minutes. Add clam juice, wine, bay leaf, salt and pepper to taste. Bring to boil, reduce heat, cover saucepan and simmer slowly for 20 minutes. Strain liquid into 2-cup measuring cup and measure. Return to saucepan and add equal amount of half and half. Warm through.

28 Crab au Gratin

Deviled Crabs

Oriental Crabmeat Salad

SALISHAN LODGE
Gleneden Beach, Oregon

2 SERVINGS

- ½ pound crabmeat, drained (rinsed with cold water if too salty), butter (as needed)
- ¼ cup Béchamel Sauce*
- ¼ cup Hollandaise Sauce (see page 176)
- 2 cups cooked rice
- ¼ pound fresh mushrooms, sliced and sautéed
- ½ cup grated medium Cheddar cheese

Preheat oven to 400°F. In 8-inch skillet, sauté crab in butter. Add Béchamel and Hollandaise Sauces to crab and heat almost to boiling point. Layer bottom of 10×6-inch baking dish with rice and mushrooms. Arrange crabmeat mixture on top. Sprinkle with cheese. Bake until cheese melts, about 10 minutes.

*Béchamel (or White) Sauce

MAKES 1 CUP

- 2 tablespoons (¼ stick) butter or margarine
- 2 tablespoons flour
- 1 cup milk
- ¼ teaspoon salt
- ⅛ teaspoon white pepper
  Dash nutmeg (optional)

Melt butter in saucepan over low heat. Add flour and blend with wire whisk. Cook 2 minutes. Add milk gradually, whisking constantly. Add salt and pepper and cook until sauce is smooth and thickened, about 5 minutes. Add nutmeg, if desired.

THE CHALFONTE
Cape May, New Jersey

6 TO 8 SERVINGS

- 1 tablespoon butter
- 1 tablespoon flour
- ½ cup half and half
- ⅛ teaspoon salt
- 1 pound crabmeat, well picked over
- 1 small onion, minced
- 1 tablespoon Worcestershire sauce
- ½ teaspoon salt
  Juice of ½ lemon
  Dash freshly ground white pepper
  Dash hot pepper sauce
- 1 cup (approximate) breadcrumbs
- 2 teaspoons paprika
- 2 tablespoons (¼ stick) butter, melted

In 2-cup saucepan, melt 1 tablespoon butter and stir in flour to make roux; gradually add half and half stirring constantly with whisk. Add ⅛ teaspoon salt and cook until sauce is thick and smooth.

Preheat oven to 400°F. In large bowl, combine crabmeat, sauce, onion, Worcestershire sauce, remaining salt, lemon juice, pepper and hot pepper sauce and mix well. Spoon crab mixture into large scallop shells or ramekins. Press mixture gently into bottom of shells. Sprinkle with breadcrumbs and paprika. Drizzle a few drops melted butter over the crumbs. Bake until top is golden brown, about 15 minutes. Serve immediately.

1770 HOUSE
East Hampton, New York

6 SERVINGS

- 1 package Japanese buckwheat noodles, cooked, drained and moistened with some sesame oil
- ½ cup alfalfa or bean sprouts
- 2 sweet red peppers, cut julienne
- 1 sweet green pepper, cut julienne
- 4 green onions, cut julienne (including 2 inches of stem)
- 2 cucumbers, peeled, seeded and cut julienne
- 1¼ cups king crabmeat (or slivered cooked chicken, pork, or other fish or meat)
- 6–10 snow peas, strings removed

DRESSING
- 1 egg
- ¾ cup corn oil
- ¼ cup Chinese sesame oil
- 2 tablespoons soy sauce
- 2 tablespoons Dijon mustard
- 1 teaspoon sugar
- 1 teaspoon lemon juice
- 1 tablespoon wine vinegar
- 1 teaspoon minced fresh garlic
- ½ teaspoon minced fresh ginger
  Salt and freshly ground pepper

Place salad ingredients in serving bowl; set aside in refrigerator.

FOR DRESSING: Beat egg in electric blender, then in steady stream slowly add half the combined oils. Add remainder by tablespoons, as in making mayonnaise. Add remaining ingredients with machine on. Adjust seasoning to taste. Pour dressing over salad, toss well and serve. If preferred, dressing may be passed at table.

PACIFIC CRAB

Usually the preparation of the continental cuisine at the City Hotel is as important as the way it is served. With this crab, however, cooking it is not a problem—eight minutes a pound in a pot of boiling court bouillon—whereas serving it is everything. The inn is situated at Columbia in California's gold country.

Artichoke and Crab

INN FOR ALL SEASONS
Scituate Harbor, Massachusetts

FOR EACH SERVING

¼ pound crabmeat, well chilled
2–3 rounded tablespoons fresh mayonnaise, well chilled
3 mushrooms, cooked, chilled and sliced
2 artichoke bottoms, cooked and chilled*
Salt and pepper
Vin Blanc Sauce (see page 27.)

In small bowl, combine crabmeat, mayonnaise and mushrooms, and spoon onto artichoke bottoms. Season to taste and serve with Vin Blanc Sauce.

* To cook 4 whole artichokes, combine 4 quarts water, 2 teaspoons salt, 4 tablespoons lemon juice and 1 tablespoon olive oil in 5-quart pan and bring to boil. Add artichokes, partially cover and simmer until bottom is tender when pierced with a fork, about 25 to 50 minutes depending on size. When cool enough to handle, pull off leaves and remove choke from bottoms.

Red Crabmeat Cakes

GATEWAYS INN
Lenox, Massachusetts

4 SERVINGS

2 cups flaked red crabmeat (snow crab, Dungeness, or king crab)
2 tablespoons whipping cream or half and half
2 eggs, beaten
1 tablespoon dry sherry
1 tablespoon minced fresh parsley
¼ teaspoon dry mustard
¼ teaspoon fresh lemon juice
Pinch thyme
Salt and pepper to taste
2 tablespoons (¼ stick) butter
2 tablespoons minced onion
2 tablespoons minced celery
½ cup soft white breadcrumbs
1 cup fine dry breadcrumbs
¼ cup (½ stick) butter

Newburg Sauce (see page 175)

In large bowl, combine crabmeat, cream, eggs, sherry, parsley, mustard, lemon juice, thyme, salt and pepper; set aside. In 8-inch skillet, melt 2 tablespoons butter, add onions and celery. Sauté until onions just turn transluscent, about 2 minutes. Do not brown. Stir in soft breadcrumbs. Add to crabmeat mixture, combining thoroughly. Chill for about 1½ hours. Form into 8 small cakes and roll in dry breadcrumbs. In 12-inch skillet, melt remaining butter and brown cakes quickly on high heat. Reduce heat and fry slowly until evenly browned, about 2 to 3 minutes on each side. Drain cakes on paper towels and serve with Newburg Sauce.

Crevettes à la Grecque

WINTER'S INN
Kingfield, Maine

FOR EACH SERVING

2 tablespoons (¼ stick) butter
½ cup small uncooked shrimp, shelled and deveined
1 garlic clove, minced
½ teaspoon chopped fresh parsley
½ tomato, diced
6 pitted black olives, sliced
3 tablespoons crumbled feta cheese

In 8-inch skillet, melt butter over medium heat. Add shrimp, garlic and parsley. Sauté until shrimp are pink but not quite done, about 1 to 2 minutes. Add tomato and black olives and sauté a few moments longer until the shrimp are opaque and pink. Transfer to small bowl. Sprinkle with cheese and serve immediately.

**A BASIC
SEAFOOD COCKTAIL SAUCE**

To serve with their outstanding
oysters, Maryland's Chesapeake House
offers this basic seafood cocktail sauce:
Blend together 7 ounces of ketchup, 1
ounce of horseradish and a few drops
of Worcestershire sauce.

30

Shrimp
and Crab Dijon

INN FOR ALL SEASONS
Scituate Harbor, Massachusetts

FOR EACH SERVING

- ¼ cup oil
- 2 large cooked crab legs or leg seg-
  ments, shelled
- 2 raw jumbo shrimp, shelled and
  deveined
  Flour
- 1 egg, beaten
  Salt and freshly ground pepper
- 1½ cups (approximate) cooked rice
  Dijon Sauce*

In heavy 8-inch skillet, heat oil to
just below smoking point. Dip crab
and shrimp in flour, then in egg;
then in flour again. Sauté quickly
just until golden, turning once. Remove with slotted spoon and arrange
on bed of rice, alternating crab and
shrimp. Top with Dijon Sauce.

*Dijon Sauce

MAKES ABOUT 2 CUPS

- 2 teaspoons Dijon mustard
  Vin Blanc Sauce (see page 27)

Add mustard to Vin Blanc Sauce and
blend gently.

Shrimp
in Beer Batter

STONEHENGE
Ridgefield, Connecticut

4 SERVINGS

BEER BATTER
- 12 ounces light domestic beer
- 1½ cups all purpose flour
- 1 tablespoon paprika
- ½ teaspoon salt

SHRIMP
- 16 raw medium shrimp, room
  temperature
  Juice of 2 lemons
  Salt and freshly ground pepper
  Worcestershire sauce
- 3–4 cups oil
- 1 cup flour

PUNGENT FRUIT SAUCE
- ¾ cup orange marmalade
- 2 tablespoons lemon juice
- 2 tablespoons orange juice
- 2 teaspoons grated horseradish
- ½ teaspoon ground ginger

FOR BATTER: Pour beer into medium bowl. Sift in flour, paprika and
salt and stir with wire whisk until
batter is light and frothy. (Batter
may be used at once or after standing
several hours. Whisk from time to
time to keep thoroughly mixed.)

FOR SHRIMP: Carefully shell
shrimp, leaving end of tail point and
flipper shell intact. Devein each
shrimp under running water. Dry
with paper towels. Place on platter
and sprinkle with lemon juice, salt,
pepper and Worcestershire sauce.
Heat oil in fryer to 375°F. Keep
temperature as constant as possible.
Dredge shrimp in flour, coating completely. Grasp each shrimp by tail
shell and dip into batter, coating
well. Drop into hot oil one by one
and cook until golden brown and
crisp. Remove with slotted spoon
and drain on paper towels. Serve
with Pungent Fruit Sauce.

FOR PUNGENT FRUIT SAUCE: Combine all ingredients in blender and
mix at low or medium speed for 1
minute.

The Old Mill Inn's way of serving clams on a tub of cracked ice is both functional and inviting.

Fresh Artichoke Bottoms with Prawns

SAN YSIDRO RANCH
Montecito, California

4 SERVINGS

¾ cup mayonnaise
¼ cup Dijon mustard
  Juice of ½ lemon
  Dash hot pepper sauce
4 medium artichokes, cooked, chokes removed (*see note page 29*)
8 butter lettuce leaves
8 very large cooked prawns or shrimp, halved lengthwise (or 16 whole medium cooked shrimp)
8 black olives
2 tomatoes, quartered
2 lemons, quartered
4 parsley sprigs

In small bowl, combine mayonnaise, mustard, lemon juice and hot pepper sauce; blend well. Fill bottom of each artichoke with mustard sauce. Arrange lettuce leaves attractively on four salad plates. Place artichoke in center of each and surround with remaining ingredients.

Shrimp Arnaud

WHEATLEIGH
Lenox, Massachusetts

6 TO 8 SERVINGS

1 cup olive oil
1 cup apple cider vinegar
1 bunch green onions, finely sliced
1 bunch parsley, finely minced
  Juice of 2 lemons
4 garlic cloves, finely minced
  Pinch salt
  White pepper
¼–½ cup Dijon mustard
2–4 tablespoons chili sauce
2–4 tablespoons mayonnaise
24 large shrimp, shelled, deveined and halved lengthwise, room temperature
1 10-ounce package or bunch fresh spinach or 1 bunch watercress
  Paprika (garnish)

In large bowl, beat oil and vinegar together with wire whisk. Add green onions, parsley, lemon juice, garlic, salt, pepper, Dijon mustard, chili sauce and mayonnaise. Add shrimp. Cover and marinate in refrigerator for several hours or overnight. To serve, place shrimp on bed of spinach or watercress. Spoon on some of marinade and sprinkle with paprika.

Lobster Florida

CHALET SUZANNE
Lake Wales, Florida

4 SERVINGS

2 grapefruit
1 cup good mayonnaise, preferably homemade
¼ cup heavy cream
¼ cup ketchup
¼ cup Cognac
2 tablespoons Madeira
1 tablespoon Worcestershire sauce
2 boiled lobsters or Florida spiny lobsters, shelled and cut in bite-sized pieces
3 tablespoons chopped fresh parsley
  Paprika

Cut grapefruit in half. Scoop out inside sections and cut into bite-sized pieces. Set aside. If desired, scallop edges of grapefruit rinds and place in cold water to keep them firm. Combine mayonnaise, cream, ketchup, Cognac, Madeira and Worcestershire sauce and blend gently. Combine lobster, grapefruit sections and sauce. Refrigerate until well chilled. Wipe grapefruit rinds dry and fill them with lobster mixture. Sprinkle with parsley and paprika and serve.

COQUILLES ST. JACQUES

Coquille is the French word for the deep shell of the scallop, or for a shell-shaped dish. It was the custom of pilgrims to the shrine of St. James of Compostela in Spain to wear a scallop shell, which probably accounts for the French name for scallop—*coquille St. Jacques* (French for St. James). Whatever the origin of the name, the popularity of this shellfish has resulted in the creation by French chefs of a variety of delectable dishes.

The European scallop differs from the American, being more delicately flavored. The best available here are the small bay scallops, which may be used in any of the French recipes. One of the most popular dishes at the Chanticleer Inn in Siasconset, Massachusetts, is the coquilles St. Jacques poached in Madeira sauce with truffles and served on a bed of spinach.

Individual Lobster Pies

PUBLICK HOUSE
Sturbridge, Massachusetts

4 SERVINGS

¼ cup (½ stick) butter
¼ cup flour
2 cups milk
2 cups half and half

¼ cup (½ stick) butter
1 pound lobster meat
½ teaspoon paprika
⅓ cup sherry
　Pinch ground red pepper
1 teaspoon salt
4 egg yolks
　Lobster Pie Topping*

In 2-quart saucepan over low heat, melt ¼ cup butter. Add flour, and beat constantly with wire whisk 2 to 3 minutes. Do not allow to color. In 1½-quart saucepan, heat milk and half and half. Gradually stir into roux and simmer over low heat for 15 minutes, stirring often. Strain to make thin cream sauce.

Preheat oven to 400°F. In 11- or 12-inch sauté pan, melt remaining butter. Add lobster meat, sprinkle with paprika and sauté over medium high heat about 5 to 7 minutes. Add ¼ cup sherry and cook 3 more minutes. Add red pepper, salt and thin cream sauce. In small bowl, stir egg yolks until thin. Stirring constantly, add 4 tablespoons hot lobster sauce to egg yolks, until well blended. Scrape yolk mixture back into pan and cook until sauce bubbles and thickens. Remove from heat and stir in remaining sherry. Spoon into 4 individual casserole dishes, distributing lobster evenly. Sprinkle with topping and bake until very brown, about 10 to 15 minutes.

*Lobster Pie Topping

4 SERVINGS

¾ cup fresh breadcrumbs
5 tablespoons (⅝ stick) butter, melted
3 tablespoons crushed potato chips
1 tablespoon freshly grated Parmesan cheese
¾ teaspoon paprika

In medium bowl, combine all ingredients and blend thoroughly.

Peruvian Ceviche of Scallops

PUMP HOUSE INN
Canadensis, Pennsylvania

6 TO 8 SERVINGS

Must be prepared at least 24 hours in advance. To be authentic, Peruvian Ceviche should be picante—spicy hot. Be sure bay scallops are very fresh. Do not use frozen sea scallops as their flavor is not delicate enough.

3 cups small fresh bay scallops (or larger scallops, cut in slices, halves or quarters)
　Juice of 3 oranges
　Juice of 2 lemons
　Juice of 2 limes
1 medium red onion, thinly sliced in rings
1 large sweet red pepper, cut into thin strips
1 large sweet green pepper, cut into thin strips
3 small shallots, minced
　Salt to taste
　Ancho chilies or ground red pepper to taste (optional)
　Oranges, lemons and limes, sliced (optional garnish)

In large bowl, thoroughly mix all ingredients except garnish and cover. Make sure all scallops are covered with citrus juice. Refrigerate for at least 24 hours, turning 3 or 4 times to ensure that marinade covers scallops evenly.

May be served in champagne glasses, scallop shells or avocado halves, and garnished with marinated onion rings and slices of orange, lemon and lime.

This dish is also a specialty at St. Orres on the northern California coast, and the version served at The Pump House Inn of Canadensis, Pennsylvania, is most unusual because of the addition of curry powder, avocado and peach.

If scallop shells large enough to hold individual servings can be found, they make an attractive presentation; otherwise ramekins may be used.

Coquilles St. Jacques Sautées au Cari

PUMP HOUSE INN
Canadensis, Pennsylvania

FOR EACH SERVING

- ¼ cup (½ stick) clarified butter
- ¾ cup bay scallops (or any small scallops) lightly dredged in flour
- 1 ounce dry sherry
- ⅜ cup whipping cream
- ½–1 teaspoon grated lemon zest or to taste
- ½–1 teaspoon grated orange zest or to taste
- ½–1 teaspoon curry powder or to taste
- 1 teaspoon shallots, minced
- ¼ ripe avocado, cubed
- ¼ ripe peach, cubed
- ½ teaspoon pimiento, chopped
  Salt and freshly ground pepper

  Orange slices (garnish)
  Lime slices (garnish)

Heat butter in 8- or 10-inch frying pan until bubbly hot but not brown or smoking. Add scallops and sauté over high flame for about 2 minutes. Remove and set aside. Add sherry and cook for 30 seconds. Add cream and grated zests and cook for 2 minutes. Add curry powder and shallots. Cook until cream has reduced, about 3 to 5 minutes. Add scallops, avocado, peach, pimiento and salt and pepper to taste. Scallops should be firm but still tender and juicy.

Serve on large platter or large scallop shells and garnish with orange and lime slices.

Seafood Salad

THE INN AT CASTLE HILL
Newport, Rhode Island

6 TO 8 SERVINGS

Prepare one day in advance.

  Court Bouillon for shellfish*
- 4 dozen bay scallops or 2 dozen sea scallops, halved
- 2 dozen frozen medium langoustines, shelled
- 2 dozen small shrimp, shelled and deveined

- 2 cups mayonnaise
- 3 tablespoons sweet sherry, or to taste
  Dill to taste, fresh if available
  Salt and pepper to taste
  Pinch nutmeg
  Dash cinnamon or to taste
  Lettuce, black olives, parsley, lemon wedges, cherry tomatoes (garnish)

In 6-quart or larger kettle, bring 4 quarts Court Bouillon to boil. Quickly add scallops, langoustines and shrimp, preferably all at once. Cover and cook over high heat for 30 seconds. Turn off heat. Keep covered until seafood is white and opaque in center but very tender, about 4 to 6 minutes. Remove seafood immediately; set aside to cool.

In large bowl, combine mayonnaise, sherry, dill, salt, pepper, nutmeg and cinnamon; blend well. Gently stir seafood into mayonnaise mixture until well dressed. Cover with plastic wrap and refrigerate overnight. Serve on bed of lettuce and garnish with olives, parsley, lemon and cherry tomatoes.

*Court Bouillon for Shellfish

MAKES 4 QUARTS

- 4–6 sprigs parsley
- 2 stalks celery with leaves attached, halved crosswise
- 1 carrot, quartered crosswise
- 1 small onion, halved
- 6 peppercorns
- 2 cloves
- 1 bay leaf
- 1½ tablespoons white wine vinegar or tarragon vinegar

Make bouquet garni by loosely wrapping all ingredients except vinegar in cheesecloth. Tie ends of cloth tightly. To 6-quart kettle containing 4 quarts water, add bouquet garni. Bring to low boil and add vinegar. Cover and simmer for 25 minutes. Discard bouquet garni.

OYSTERS A LA GINO

Oysters à la Gino is a new twist to baked stuffed oysters and was developed by Ken and Wendy Gibson, innkeepers at the Robert Morris Inn. The Gibsons zealously guarded their recipe for many years until they had a change of heart and made it public. The Robert Morris Inn is located on Maryland's Chesapeake Bay by the Bellevue-Oxford ferry, which is said to be the oldest continuously operating private ferry in the United States.

Chicken and Baby Lobster in Cream Sauce

L'HOSTELLERIE BRESSANE
Hillsdale, New York

2 SERVINGS

- 3 tablespoons (⅜ stick) butter
- 1 whole breast from 3-pound chicken, split and boned except for wing bones
  Salt and white pepper
- 1 teaspoon diced onion
- ¼ cup dry white wine
- 1 cup whipping cream
- 2 baby lobster or crayfish tail, cut and opened on underside

In 8- or 10-inch skillet, melt butter over low heat; do not allow to brown. Season chicken with salt and pepper to taste and cook over low to medium heat, covered, for 10 to 12 minutes, turning frequently. Chicken must remain white. Add onion. Sauté for 2 minutes over high heat. Pour off butter. Add wine and reduce over low heat until wine has completely evaporated. Add cream and simmer uncovered until thickened, about 5 minutes. Add lobster; cook until it just turns pink. Taste for seasoning. Serve immediately.

Fish Balls

PHILBROOK FARM
Shelburne, New Hampshire

3 TO 4 SERVINGS

Prepare a day in advance.

- 2 cups peeled and cubed potatoes
- 1 cup cubed salt cod

- 1 egg
- 1 teaspoon butter
  Salt and freshly ground pepper
  Oil for deep frying

Combine potatoes and salt cod in bowl. Cover with water and soak overnight. Drain completely. Transfer potatoes and fish to 2-quart saucepan and cover with fresh water. Bring to boil and cook over medium heat until potatoes are tender, about 20 minutes. Drain well. Mash potatoes and fish together.

Preheat oil in deep fryer, heavy saucepan or skillet to 375°F. Beat egg and add to fish mixture together with butter, salt and pepper, mixing well. Drop by tablespoon into hot oil and fry until nicely golden brown, about 5 minutes. Remove with skimmer or slotted spoon, drain on paper towels and serve immediately.

Ben Franklin's Smoked Oysters and Lamb

BLACK BASS HOTEL
Lumberville, Pennsylvania

4 TO 6 SERVINGS

- 2 strips bacon, diced
- ½ onion, minced
- 2 tablespoons flour
- 2 pounds choice lamb leg, boned, cubed and trimmed of fat
- 1½ cups brown lamb stock
- 1 can whole smoked oysters
- ¼ cup white wine
- 1½ teaspoons tomato paste
- 1 teaspoon sage
- 1 teaspoon Worcestershire sauce
  Salt and pepper to taste

Preheat oven to 400°F. In 12-inch skillet, fry bacon until it begins to lightly brown. Add onion and sauté over moderately high heat until soft, about 5 minutes. Remove bacon and onion from pan with slotted spatula; set aside. Do not remove fat from skillet. Sprinkle flour on lamb and sauté in skillet until tender. In shallow roasting pan combine bacon, onion, lamb stock, oysters, wine, tomato paste, sage, Worcestershire sauce, salt and pepper. Add lamb, baste with liquid and bake until heated throughout, approximately 10 minutes.

SHUCKING OYSTERS

The trick to opening oysters is to twist your way in until the opening is found. Brute force just doesn't do the job, according to Captain Buddy Harrison, pictured at left, who is skipper of a commercial fishing fleet headquartered at Maryland's Chesapeake House on Chesapeake Bay, one of America's great fishing grounds.

Oysters à la Gino

ROBERT MORRIS INN
Oxford, Maryland

4 TO 6 SERVINGS

- 1 cup Newburg Sauce (*see page* 175)
- 2 tablespoons dry or medium sherry, or to taste
- 3 strips bacon, cooked crisp and crumbled fine
- ¼ teaspoon garlic powder
  Dash Worcestershire sauce
  Pinch salt or to taste
  Freshly ground pepper to taste
- 1 1-pound can lump crabmeat, flaked
- 24 oysters, shucked and returned to bottom shells
- 2 cups (approximate) fresh bread-crumbs
- ½ cup (1 stick) butter, melted
- ¼ cup paprika
- 6 strips bacon, quartered

Preheat oven to 450°F. In large bowl combine Newburg Sauce, sherry, crumbled bacon, garlic powder, Worcestershire sauce, salt and pepper. Mix well. Gently fold in crabmeat. Place oysters on baking sheet. Fill each oyster with equal portions of crab mixture. In medium bowl, combine and mix bread-crumbs, butter and paprika. Mixture should be consistency of thick paste. Spoon heaping teaspoon over top of each oyster, mounding well. Top with uncooked bacon. Bake until bacon is cooked, about 10 minutes. If necessary, place the oysters under hot broiler to crisp bacon. Serve immediately.

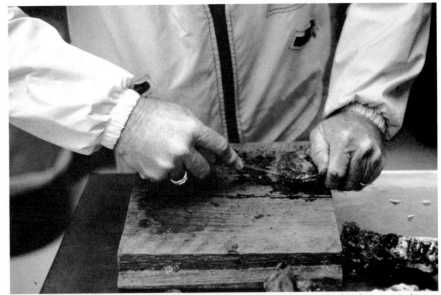

Hold oyster curved side down with hinge pointing away. Insert the knife at a 45-degree angle, about halfway between the hinge and lip, by twisting the blade back and forth until the juices seep out and the opening becomes evident.

After pushing the blade in with a twisting motion, rotate the knife toward yourself, sweeping it along the underside of top shell to cut the muscle from the top of shell.

Lever shell open, smooth out top of oyster with blade and serve immediately in bottom half with a choice of fresh lemon and seafood cocktail sauce.

36 Bacon and Fish Rolls

THE MAINSTAY
Cape May, New Jersey

6 SERVINGS

6 ¼-pound flounder or sole fillets
2 tablespoons fresh lemon juice
  Seasoned salt
6 slices bacon, cooked until not quite crisp
1 lemon, cut into 6 wedges

Preheat oven to 350°F. Sprinkle fish with lemon juice and salt. Roll up each fillet and wrap bacon around outside of each. Place in greased shallow baking pan and bake until fish is tender, about 15 minutes. Serve with lemon wedge.

Wine-Baked Country Ham

PILGRIM'S INN
Deer Isle, Maine

20 SERVINGS

May need to begin preparation 2 days in advance. Serve with spoon bread or scalloped potatoes.

1 12–14-pound country or Smithfield ham
4 cups ginger wine (or cider or beer)
½ cup bourbon
  Brown sugar (optional)
  Fruit (optional garnish)

Follow directions on label for preparing country ham for cooking or soak Smithfield ham in cold water to cover for 12 to 24 hours. Change water several times. Scrub ham with brush under running water and wipe with damp cloth. Do not boil or simmer ham.

In shallow roasting pan, place ham on enough heavy-duty foil to make a roomy envelope for ham. Add ginger wine (or cider or beer) and seal foil. Put ham in cold oven. Heat oven to 475°F and roast ham for 35 minutes. Turn off heat and let ham cool in oven for 2 to 4 hours. Repeat baking method and leave in oven for 4 to 5 hours, or overnight. Discard foil and drippings, keeping ham in roasting pan. Score fat in diamonds or squares and heat ham in oven at 350°F until surface is quite hot, about 15 minutes. Remove to top of stove. In 1-cup saucepan, heat bourbon. Pour over ham, ignite and flame. If desired, glaze ham with brown sugar and/or garnish with favorite fruit.

Meatballs

THE HOMESTEAD
Sugar Hill, New Hampshire

MAKES 60 TO 70 MEATBALLS

These can be used as an hors d'oeuvre, or as a main course covered with tomato sauce or brown gravy and served with rice or noodles. They also freeze well.

2 pounds lean beef, finely ground
1 cup dry breadcrumbs
½ cup freshly grated Parmesan cheese
2 eggs
1 teaspoon salt
½ teaspoon garlic powder
½ teaspoon dried oregano
  Freshly ground pepper to taste
¼ cup olive oil

In large bowl, combine all ingredients except oil; blend thoroughly. Use 1 tablespoon of mixture to form each ball. In 12-inch skillet, heat the olive oil and fit only half as many meatballs as skillet can hold (this leaves room for turning). Sauté until evenly browned on outside and cooked but still juicy in center (cut one open and taste to test doneness). Remove with slotted spoon and drain on paper towels.

George and Eleanor Pavloff, the innkeepers at Pilgrim's Inn, Deer Isle, Maine, offer sophisticated accommodations at an inn that is heated entirely by stones and fireplaces, just as it was two centuries ago. Former Vice-President and Mrs. Mondale, personal friends of the Pavloffs, attended the opening reception at the time the Pavloffs acquired the inn. Mr. Mondale's favorite dish, Fritz Grits, is served regularly, and that recipe, among many others, is included in this collection.

Beef Miroton

PHILBROOK FARM INN
Shelburne, New Hampshire

4 SERVINGS

- 4 thick 4–6-ounce slices leftover pot roast, steak or roast beef
- 2 large onions, finely chopped
- 3 tablespoons (⅜ stick) butter, melted
- 1 tablespoon flour
- 1 cup beef stock
- 2 tablespoons vinegar
- 2 tablespoons tomato paste or catsup
  Salt and pepper to taste
  Pinch garlic powder
  Breadcrumbs
  Parmesan cheese, grated

Trim all fat and gristle from beef slices and set aside. In 8-inch skillet, sauté onions in butter until tender and golden. Stir flour in thoroughly. Add beef stock, vinegar and tomato paste or catsup. Season with salt, pepper and garlic. Simmer, covered, until flavors are blended, about 20 minutes.

Preheat oven to 350°F. Pour half of sauce into shallow baking dish. Top with beef slices and cover with remaining sauce. Sprinkle with breadcrumbs and cheese. Bake until topping is brown and sauce is bubbly, about 10 minutes.

Tourtière

PUBLICK HOUSE
Sturbridge, Massachusetts

6 SERVINGS

- Pastry for two 9-inch piecrusts (*see page 176*)
- 1 pound ground lean pork
- 1 pound ground lean beef
- 1 medium onion, minced
- 2 cups Brown Sauce (*see page 175*)
- 1 teaspoon cinnamon
- ¼ teaspoon ground cloves
- ¾ cup soft breadcrumbs
- 1 cup diced cooked potatoes
  Salt and pepper
- 1 egg, beaten

Preheat oven to 375°F. Roll half of pastry on floured work surface and line 9-inch pie pan. Set aside. In 12-inch sauté pan, sauté pork, beef and onion on medium-high heat until browned, about 10 minutes. Pour off fat. Add sauce, cinnamon and cloves, and simmer for 5 minutes. Stir in breadcrumbs, potatoes, salt and pepper to taste. Blend well and remove from heat. Spoon mixture into pastry-lined pie pan. Roll out remaining pastry and gently lay over pie pan. Seal and crimp edges. Brush with beaten egg. Bake in lower third of oven until browned, about 45 minutes.

Tomato and Zucchini Pie

PILGRIM'S INN
Deer Isle, Maine

4 TO 6 SERVINGS

- 2 cups sliced small zucchini, ends discarded
- 1 small onion, thinly sliced
- 3 tablespoons (⅜ stick) butter
- 4 tablespoons olive oil
- 1–2 tomatoes, thinly sliced
  Salt and pepper
- ½ teaspoon oregano
- 2 eggs, beaten
- ¾ cup milk
- ½ cup sour cream
- 1 tablespoon flour
- ¼ cup shredded Swiss cheese
- ¼ cup grated Parmesan cheese
- ¼ cup cracker crumbs

In 10-inch skillet, sauté zucchini and onion for 5 minutes in 1½ tablespoons butter and 2 tablespoons olive oil; remove and set aside. In remaining butter and olive oil, sauté tomatoes. Add salt, pepper and oregano to taste. Sauté until lightly browned; set aside. In medium mixing bowl, mix together eggs, milk, sour cream and flour.

Preheat oven to 350°F. In greased 2-quart baking dish, layer zucchini-onion mixture and tomatoes. Pour egg mixture over top. In small bowl, mix together Swiss cheese, Parmesan cheese and cracker crumbs and sprinkle on top. Bake until pie is puffed and golden brown, about 30 minutes.

NOTE: Experiment by sprinkling caraway seeds or other spices between layers of this savory pie.

THE MAINSTAY

Tom and Sue Carroll are the innkeepers of the Mainstay Inn, a perfectly preserved Victorian residence in Cape May, New Jersey, a community known for having the largest single concentration of Victorian homes in America. Although the inn has no restaurant, marvelous breakfasts are served to the guests. Strawberry crêpes, cheese strata, fried apples and bacon and fish rolls are some of the delicacies, and the recipes are all included here.

38 Ham and Apple Pie

THE MAINSTAY
Cape May, New Jersey

6 SERVINGS

- 6–8 large tart apples, peeled and thinly sliced
- ½ pound cooked ham, diced
- ¾ cup brown sugar
- 2 tablespoons flour
- ½ teaspoon salt
- ½ teaspoon freshly ground pepper
  Pastry*

Preheat oven to 325°F. Grease a 10-inch glass pie dish. Cover bottom with one-third of apple slices. Layer with half amount of ham. Sprinkle with half each of sugar, flour, salt and pepper. Layer with another third of apples and remaining ham and seasonings. Top with remaining apples. Cover with pastry. Trim and seal edges. Pierce crust with fork to let steam escape. Bake until apples are tender, sugar is melted and top is lightly browned, about 1½ hours.

*Pastry

MAKES 10-INCH CRUST

- 1 cup flour
- ½ teaspoon salt
- ½ cup shortening
- 2½ tablespoons cold water

In medium bowl, combine flour and salt. Cut in shortening with pastry blender or two knives until mixture is consistency of coarse meal. Sprinkle with water a teaspoon at a time and lightly mix with fork after each addition. Handle pastry as little as possible. Quickly form into ball and wrap in waxed paper. Refrigerate at least 1 hour. Roll out on floured surface into round about ⅛ inch thick, and 1 inch larger than overall size of pie dish.

Ham and Mushroom Casserole

CAPTAIN WHIDBEY INN
Coupeville, Washington

8 TO 10 SERVINGS

- 3 cups dry breadcrumbs
- 2 cups (4 sticks) butter, melted
- 1 cup flour
- 4 cups milk
- ½ cup sherry
- ½ teaspoon white pepper
  Salt
- 12 hard-cooked eggs, sliced
- 1 pound fresh whole mushrooms
- 3 cups ham cut in ½-inch cubes

In 10-inch skillet, toast breadcrumbs in 1 cup melted butter until golden. In 2-quart saucepan, make roux with remaining butter and flour. Add milk and sherry all at once. Stir and cook until thickened. Add pepper and salt to taste.

Preheat oven to 350°F. Cover bottom of 12 × 8 × 4-inch baking dish with half breadcrumbs. Layer eggs, mushrooms, ham and sherry sauce and top with remaining breadcrumbs. Bake until heated through, about 30 minutes.

DINNER

In most country inns guests look to dinner as the event of the evening, and innkeepers rise to the occasion not only in the food they serve but also in the way they present it. As Elaine Wondolowski of the Inn for All Seasons in Scituate Harbor, Massachusetts, puts it: "The entire production, as in a well-performed symphony, must be perfectly balanced, precisely delivered, aesthetically appealing and, above all, delectable."

Today's gourmet dinners comprise a few courses impeccably prepared. Table appointments are as attractive as the food itself, with sparkling glassware, crisp linen and fresh flowers. At the Inn at Castle Hill, Newport, Rhode Island, each table is set with a distinctive china pattern. Each setting is different at Florida's Chalet Suzanne—nothing matches but everything fits. At the 1970s' St. Orres on the California coast, meals are served on stoneware thrown by a local potter, while the mid-nineteenth-century Marshlands Inn uses Spode china and the family's own silverware for its regional fare.

40 Roast Beef

New England Boiled Dinner

RED FOX TAVERN
Middleburg, Virginia

4 TO 6 SERVINGS

Roast beef is at its succulent best when served rare. Those who prefer well-done beef should pot roast a cheaper cut.

4 TO 6 SERVINGS

1 4–5-pound standing rib roast (or rolled rib roast)

Garlic powder to taste
Salt and pepper to taste

Preheat oven to 325°F. Wipe roast with damp paper towels. Sprinkle roast with garlic powder, salt and pepper. Place fat side up on rack in large shallow roasting pan. Insert meat thermometer into center of thickest part of meat and roast uncovered. For very rare: 130°F on thermometer or 15 to 17 minutes per pound. For medium rare: 150°F on thermometer or 18 to 20 minutes per pound. For those who must have it well done: 165°F on thermometer or 22 to 28 minutes per pound. When roast is done, remove from oven and let stand 20 minutes before carving.

THE HOMESTEAD
Sugar Hill, New Hampshire

6 TO 8 SERVINGS

The Homestead recommends Indian Pudding (*recipe page* 172) for dessert.

MEAT

1 4–5-pound corned beef brisket, fat removed

VEGETABLES

8 large carrots, halved
6 turnips, peeled, halved and cut into 1-inch-thick slices
6 potatoes, scrubbed and cut into 1-inch-thick slices
2 cups dried white haricot or navy beans, presoaked
2 large firm cabbages, cored and quartered
8–10 whole beets
¼ cup (½ stick) butter, melted

FOR MEAT: Place brisket in a large pot and barely cover with water. Cover tightly and bring to a boil. Reduce heat and allow to simmer until the meat is fork tender, about 3 hours. Add more boiling water if needed. Turn off heat and allow meat to remain in liquid until 1½ hours before serving. Then, remove meat and wrap it in foil to keep warm.

FOR VEGETABLES: After meat is removed, add carrots, turnips and potatoes to liquid in pot. Place presoaked beans in cheesecloth and hang, covered by liquid, over the edge of pot. Bring to boil, then reduce heat, cover and simmer until tender, about 15 to 25 minutes. Cook beets separately, peel and add to pot just before serving.

To serve, cut slab of brisket into long, thin slices and arrange down middle of large platter. Arrange vegetables on either side of meat and brush melted butter over top.

NOTE: A dish called Red Flannel Hash can be made from leftovers. Put whatever is left in a meat grinder. Add butter or bacon fat to a skillet and sauté hash until heated through. Serve with a salad and sour pickles.

CARL LUTZ, LOGAN INN

Carl Lutz, co-owner of the Logan Inn, has been a gourmet enthusiast for as far back as he can remember, enjoying a good cookbook as much as a good novel. The menu reflects some of his latest food finds such as roast loin of pork with prunes as well as favorites from his grandmother's kitchen. When Carl is not in the kitchen adding another caper to the sauce, or showing his guests around the oldest building in town, he's busy being mayor of New Hope, the historic Pennsylvania town where Logan Inn is located.

Viennese Boiled Beef with Caper Sauce

LOGAN INN
New Hope, Pennsylvania

6 SERVINGS

- 3–4 pounds top round of beef (or brisket), trimmed of all fat
  Boiling water to cover meat
  Salt and freshly ground pepper
- 6–8 small whole carrots, peeled
- 6–8 small onions
- 6–8 small white turnips, peeled
- 2 small parsnips, cut in 3 pieces each
- 6–8 small new potatoes, boiled (optional)
  Caper Sauce*

Place beef in Dutch oven and cover with boiling water. Add salt and pepper to taste. Bring to brisk simmer and cover. Cook over low heat for approximately 2 hours.

Add carrots, onions, turnips and parsnips and continue cooking until meat can easily be pierced with long-tined kitchen fork or skewer, about 2 more hours.

Serve meat surrounded with vegetables from stock and small boiled new potatoes, if desired. Serve Caper Sauce separately. (Remainder of stock makes delicious soup base.)

*Caper Sauce

MAKES ABOUT 2 CUPS

- 4 tablespoons (½ stick) butter
- 4 tablespoons flour
- 2 cups of strained defatted meat stock, boiling
- 1 tablespoon grated horseradish or to taste
- 4–6 ounces capers, juice included

Melt butter in 1 quart saucepan and add flour. Blend completely for 1 minute without browning. Add boiling stock all at once and beat with whisk until smooth and thickened. Add horseradish and enough capers and juice from jar to give sauce plenty of snap. Blend gently.

Filet de Boeuf Wellington

41

COPPER BEECH INN
Ivoryton, Connecticut

8 SERVINGS

PÂTÉ
- 1 pound pork
- 12 ounces veal
- 8 ounces duck liver
- 3 eggs
- 2 ounces Cognac
- ½ medium onion
- 3 teaspoons seasoned salt
- 1 tablespoon freshly ground pepper
- ½ teaspoon dry mustard
- ¼ teaspoon garlic powder
- ½ teaspoon poultry seasoning
- 8–10 strips bacon

SAUCE PÉRIGOURDINE
- 1 quart veal stock
- ½ cup Madeira wine
- 2 tablespoons foie gras, chopped
- 4 tablespoons truffles, chopped
  Juice from truffle

BEEF
- 1 4-pound center cut filet mignon, trimmed of fat (tenderloin), room temperature
- 4 tablespoons oil
  Salt and pepper
- 1 pound Puff Pastry*
- 1 egg, beaten
  Watercress (garnish)

FOR PÂTÉ: Put all ingredients except bacon through meat grinder twice. Line bottom and sides of 2-quart loaf pan with some of bacon strips. Preheat oven to 350°F. Fill

pan with pâté mixture and cover with remaining bacon. Bake for 1 hour and 10 to 15 minutes in hot water bath. Remove from oven and cool. There will be a large portion of leftover pâté. Use as hors d'oeuvre, appetizer served with cornichons or in other recipes.

FOR SAUCE: In 2-quart pan, bring veal stock to boil, then simmer until reduced by half. In small pan, heat Madeira until reduced to syrupy consistency. Add to veal stock. Add foie gras, truffles and truffle juice.

FOR BEEF: Preheat oven to 400°F. Sear beef in hot oil on all sides for about 5 minutes in all. Cool. Sprinkle with salt and pepper. Cover top of filet with ⅛-inch-thick layer of pâté. Roll out refrigerated puff pastry and wrap filet in puff pastry. Place seam side down on a cookie sheet. Brush pastry lightly with beaten egg. Allow to dry and brush again with egg wash. If the first application of egg wash does not dry in 5 to 10 minutes, place Wellington in refrigerator for 5 minutes to dry. Bake 45 minutes for rare. Cool 10 minutes before slicing. Serve slices of filet on top of Périgourdine sauce and garnish with watercress.

*Puff Pastry

MAKES ABOUT 2 POUNDS

4½–5 cups all purpose flour
  1 teaspoon salt
1⅓ cups (approximate) water
  1 pound (4 sticks) sweet butter

Put 4 cups flour in large mixing bowl. Make well in center, add salt and 1 cup water. Mix flour and water together to make a firm, slightly sticky dough. Add additional water gradually if needed. Form dough into ball, turn out on table and knead until smooth and elastic, about 15 to 20 minutes. Refrigerate dough in plastic bag for 30 minutes.

When dough is chilled, roll out on well-floured board or pastry cloth to rectangle about 8 × 18 inches. Cut butter into thin squares and place on top two-thirds of dough. Fold bottom third of dough halfway over butter, then fold buttered section down over bottom section. Roll dough again into rectangle. If butter breaks through dough while rolling, flour broken places well. Fold ends of rectangle to meet in center. Fold dough in half (like closing a book) twice more, making 4 layers. Refrigerate well covered for 1 hour before rolling again. Repeat rolling, folding and refrigerating three more times. Dough should be rested, well covered in refrigerator for at least 2 hours before final rolling into desired shape and thickness.

Individual Beef Wellingtons

ST. ORRES
Gualala, California

6 SERVINGS

PÂTÉ
  1 pound fresh mushrooms
  ⅓ pound ham
  ½ cup (1 stick) butter
  1 tablespoon chopped shallots
  1 tablespoon marjoram
  1 teaspoon black pepper
  ¼ teaspoon nutmeg
  ½ cup Demi-glace (Brown Sauce, see page 175)

PASTRY
  1 pound Puff Pastry (purchase ready made or see recipe opposite)

BEEF
  6 7-ounce beef tenderloin fillets, well trimmed
    Oil

EGG WASH
  1 egg yolk
  1 tablespoon water
  1 tablespoon cream
    Pinch salt

SAUCE
  1 tablespoon chopped shallots
  ¼ pound mushrooms, sliced
  ⅓ cup Madeira
  1 cup Demi-glace
    Salt and pepper

FOR PÂTÉ: Grind mushrooms and ham with medium blade of food grinder. In 10-inch skillet over medium heat, sauté mushrooms and

THE COPPER BEECH

The Copper Beech Inn is a Connecticut mansion whose every detail has an elegant touch. The inn's former owner was an ivory merchant who spent a lifetime collecting and enjoying fine accoutrements to his exotic lifestyle, and the inn seems dedicated to his way of life. Double tapered rolled linen napkins are just one item that set off the inn's outstanding French cuisine.

Beef Burgundy

Beef Stroganoff

ham lightly in butter. Add shallots, marjoram, pepper, nutmeg and Demi-glace. Mix well to coat ingredients with Demi-glace and continue to cook, stirring constantly until Demi-glace is almost dry but mushroom mixture still binds together.

FOR PASTRY: Roll out ⅛-inch thick. Cut into 6 equal rectangles. Use trimmings to form flowers, leaves, etc., to decorate tops of Wellingtons. Chill squares and decorations until ready to use.

FOR BEEF: In 12-inch skillet, sauté fillets in oil to just below desired doneness. Remove fillets to large baking sheet and chill until ready to use. Reserve pan juices in skillet. Preheat oven to 450°F. Cover tops of fillets with pâté. Invert each fillet in center of puff pastry rectangle and enclose completely with pastry. Place seam side down on baking pan.

FOR EGG WASH: In small bowl beat together egg yolk, water, cream and salt. Brush pastry-covered beef with egg wash. Decorate with pastry trimmings and brush again with egg wash. Bake until nicely browned, about 10 minutes.

FOR SAUCE: Using skillet containing reserved pan juices, add shallots, mushrooms and Madeira. Simmer until mushrooms are cooked. Add Demi-glace, simmer 1 minute and season to taste. To serve, place tablespoon of sauce on each plate and individual beef Wellingtons on sauce.

NEW LONDON INN
New London, New Jersey

4 TO 6 SERVINGS

    4 tablespoons (approximate) margarine or vegetable oil
    5 medium onions, diced
    ½ pound mushrooms, sliced
    2 pounds lean boneless beef chuck
    1½ tablespoons flour
    1 teaspoon salt
    ¼ teaspoon marjoram
    ¼ teaspoon thyme
    ⅛ teaspoon freshly ground black pepper
    ¾ cup beef stock or canned beef bouillon
    1½ cups Burgundy
 8–10 cups cooked rice or noodles, hot

In 11-inch skillet or 9-inch sauté pan, heat 2 tablespoons margarine or oil and add onions and mushrooms. Cook, stirring occasionally, until onions are tender but not browned. Drain off liquid and remove onions and mushrooms from skillet; set aside. Cut meat into 1-inch cubes. Add more margarine or oil to skillet, if needed, and brown beef cubes. In small bowl, mix together flour, salt, marjoram, thyme and pepper. Sprinkle over meat, stirring to coat all sides. Add stock or bouillon, cover and simmer until meat is tender, about 1½ to 2 hours. Stir in Burgundy, onions and mushrooms and reheat. Serve over rice or noodles.

PILGRIM'S INN
Deer Isle, Maine

12 TO 14 SERVINGS

Especially good served with tomato aspic* and a salad of young spinach leaves or other greens.

    4 pounds sirloin tip, trimmed of fat
    ½ cup (1 stick) butter
    3 large Spanish onions, chopped
    2 4-ounce cans mushroom pieces, juice reserved, or 1 pound fresh mushrooms, chopped
    4 tablespoons flour
    ¾ cup tomato juice
    2 garlic cloves, minced
    3 large bay leaves, crumbled
       Salt to taste
    3 tablespoons Hungarian paprika, or to taste
    2 cups sour cream
    1 16-ounce package noodles or 3½ cups rice, cooked

Cut sirloin tip into ½-inch-thick slices; cut slices into thin, finger-sized strips; set aside. In 12-inch heavy skillet, melt ¼ cup butter and sauté onions and mushrooms until tender but not browned. With slotted spoon transfer onions and mushrooms to 5- or 6-quart pot. Reserve liquid. Wipe out skillet. In small bowl, blend flour with tomato juice. If using canned mushrooms, blend reserved mushroom juice into tomato juice. Add to onions and mushrooms and stir. Melt remaining butter in skillet and brown beef strips rapidly, a handful at a time. As meat is browning, stir in garlic, bay leaves, salt and paprika. When all strips are browned, add to onion mixture in pot together with reserved pan juices

RIGHT:
Individual Beef Wellingtons
from St. Orres Inn, Gualala, California.
See page 42.
OVERLEAF:
Filet de Boeuf Wellington
from the Copper Beech Inn, Ivoryton, Connecticut.
See page 41.

DINNER

44

Farmer's Stew

THE HOMESTEAD
Sugar Hill, New Hampshire

and brown bits scraped from skillet. Cook over low heat, stirring frequently, until meat is tender. Stir in sour cream, taste and adjust seasoning. Simmer until heated thoroughly. Serve over noodles or rice.

*Tomato Aspic

12 TO 14 SERVINGS

- 1 quart tomato juice
- 2 tablespoons unflavored gelatin
  Lemon juice to taste
  Hot pepper sauce to taste
  Worcestershire sauce to taste
- 4 ounces cream cheese
- 2 tablespoons light cream
- ½ cup walnut or pecan pieces
- ½ teaspoon sugar

Pour 1 cup tomato juice into small bowl, add gelatin and allow to soften. In 1½-quart saucepan, heat remaining tomato juice. Add lemon juice, hot pepper sauce and Worcestershire sauce. Add tomato juice-gelatin mixture and stir until gelatin is completely dissolved. Allow to cool to lukewarm. Pour about half into 1½-quart mold or use smaller individual molds filling them half full. Refrigerate until partially set. Put cream cheese, cream, nuts and sugar into blender or processor and blend thoroughly. Spoon into center of mold and cover with remaining gelatin mixture. Refrigerate until firm. Unmold before serving.

4 SERVINGS

The addition of dumplings makes this a perfect meal when accompanied with a fresh green salad and followed by a piece of apple pie.

- 1 2-inch cube salt pork, cut into ¼-inch dice
- 2 pounds lean beef chuck, cut into ½-inch cubes
- 6 carrots, sliced into rounds
- 6 medium potatoes, cut into bite-sized pieces
- 3 large onions, sliced
- 3 quarts water
  Salt and pepper

  Homestead dumplings*

In 12-inch skillet, sauté salt pork until fat is rendered. Add beef and sauté on high heat until brown on all sides. Place carrots, potatoes, onions, beef and rendered salt pork into 6-quart kettle. Add water and simmer, covered, until beef is tender and flavor of broth is satisfactory, about 60 minutes. Season with salt and pepper to taste. Add Homestead dumplings during final 20 minutes of stew cooking time. (It is not necessary to thicken stew, as it will absorb some of flour from dumplings.)

*Homestead Dumplings

4 SERVINGS

- 2 cups flour
- 4 teaspoons baking powder
- 1 teaspoon sugar
- 1 teaspoon salt
- 1 cup milk

In medium bowl, sift together flour, baking powder, sugar and salt. Add milk, stirring until batter can be rounded on a wet tablespoon. Bring stew to fast rolling boil. Drop batter by the tablespoon into stew. Cook 5 minutes uncovered. Cover tightly, reduce heat slightly and cook for 15 minutes more without lifting cover.

Veal Medallions from Town Farms Inn, Middletown, Connecticut. *See page* 65.

Rabbit Casserole from Town Farms Inn, Middletown, Connecticut. *See page* 71.

OVERLEAF:
Roast Beef
from the Red Fox Tavern,
Middleburg, Virginia.
See page 40.

Chicken Oriental from Saxtons River Inn, Saxtons River, Vermont. *See page* 73.

Chicken Luau from Chalet Suzanne, Lake Wales, Florida. *See page* 75.

OVERLEAF:
New England Boiled Dinner
from The Homestead,
Sugar Hill, New Hampshire.
See page 40.

Chicken Ridgefield, The Elms, Ridgefield, Connecticut. *See page* 75.

Mussels in Cream
from Town Farms Inn,
Middletown, Connecticut.
See page 90.

Boiled Maine Lobsters,
ready for eating,
photographed at
the Whitehall Inn,
Camden, Maine.

Barbara and Gerry Liebert are transplanted New Yorkers who brought new life to the backwoods of Vermont with their first venture into innkeeping—the Tulip Tree Inn. Their reputation became established within a year of converting a Chittenden, Vermont, summer home into a typical New England country inn. The food was certainly one of the main attractions, and Barbara kept a record of the menus to make sure repeat visitors got different gourmet meals each time. Since this auspicious beginning, the Lieberts, along with their daughter and son-in-law, have become the proprietors of the Windflower Inn in Great Barrington, Massachusetts. This larger establishment affords more guests an opportunity to sample the Lieberts' excellent cuisine.

61

Daube of Beef Provençale

L'HOSTELLERIE BRESSANE
Hillsdale, New York

6 TO 8 SERVINGS

- 3 pounds lean stewing beef, cut in 2-inch cubes
- ½ pound salt pork, sliced
- 4 carrots, peeled and sliced in rounds
- 4 tomatoes, mashed
- ½ pound mushrooms, quartered
- 4 garlic cloves, minced
- 4 bay leaves
- 12 black olives
- ½ cup chopped fresh parsley
  Salt and pepper
- 1 large onion, thinly sliced
- ½ cup brandy
- 2 quarts (approximate) Chablis
- 1 cup beef bouillon or veal stock

Preheat oven to 300°F. In a 7- to 8-quart ovenproof pot or casserole, add ingredients in following order: stewing beef, salt pork, carrots, tomatoes, mushrooms, garlic, bay leaves, black olives, chopped parsley, salt and pepper to taste, onion and brandy. Pour wine to about 3 inches above ingredients. Add bouillon or stock, cover tightly and bring to boil. Place in oven, keep covered and simmer until beef is tender, about 2½ to 3 hours.

Ragoût de Boulettes (Meatball Stew)

HOVEY MANOR
North Hatley, Québec, Canada

8 TO 10 SERVINGS

- 3 pounds ground beef
- 1 tablespoon salt
- 1 tablespoon freshly ground black pepper
  Cinnamon
  Cloves
  Flour
  Oil
- 8–10 small potatoes, sliced
- 8–10 small whole carrots
- 5 cups Brown Sauce (*see page 175*), or beef bouillon
  Thyme to taste

In large bowl, mix ground beef with half the salt and pepper. Add cinnamon and cloves to taste. Form into balls and roll lightly in flour. In large skillet, add enough oil to cover bottom and fry ⅓ of balls at a time until brown.

In covered 6-quart saucepan, simmer potatoes and carrots in water to cover until partially cooked, about 15 minutes. Drain. Add vegetables to meatballs in skillet. Stir in Brown Sauce or bouillon, thyme and remaining salt and pepper. Cook uncovered until vegetables are tender and sauce is thick.

Short Ribs

WINDFLOWER INN
Great Barrington, Massachusetts

4 TO 6 SERVINGS

- 4–5 pounds beef short ribs
- 2 large onions, chopped
- 1 cup dry red wine
- ⅔ cup catsup
- 3 tablespoons soy sauce
- 2 tablespoons brown sugar, firmly packed
- ½ teaspoon pepper

Preheat oven to 425°F. Without added fat, in hot Dutch oven, brown short ribs over medium-high heat, about 10 minutes. In bowl, combine remaining ingredients and pour over ribs. Cover and bake until tender and meat starts to separate from bone, about 1 hour 15 minutes. Remove ribs to platter and set aside. Cool sauce until fat congeals on surface and remove fat. When ready to serve, return ribs to sauce and heat in slow to moderate oven (300°F) until hot.

OPPOSITE:
Short Ribs
from the Windflower Inn,
Great Barrington, Massachusetts.

62 Bavarian Liver Schnitzel

KEDRON VALLEY INN
South Woodstock, Vermont

4 SERVINGS

- 1 pound liver (calves or beef), thinly sliced and cut in ½-inch strips
  Salt and pepper to taste
- 1½ cups (approximately) flour
- 2 tablespoons (approximately) shortening
- 1 tablespoon butter
- 1 tablespoon flour
- ½ cup beef stock
- ½ cup finely chopped onions
- 1 cup red wine

Season liver with salt and pepper and dredge with flour. Sauté rapidly in shortening over high heat until well browned but pink inside. Remove liver and keep warm. In a saucepan, melt butter, add flour and cook gently until golden brown. Add stock and make sauce by simmering, whisking until well blended, about 2 to 3 minutes. Sauté onions in liver pan over medium heat until lightly browned, about 5 minutes. Add wine and sauce to onions and simmer for 5 minutes. Add sautéed liver and heat 1 minute more.

Calf's Liver Alpina

SAXTONS RIVER INN
Saxtons River, Vermont

6 SERVINGS

- 3 pounds calf's liver, membrane removed, thinly sliced on diagonal into 12 thin slices
- 1 cup milk
- 3 tablespoons (⅜ stick) butter, melted
- 1 tablespoon flour
- 2 heaping tablespoons chopped fresh chives
- 1 heaping tablespoon chopped fresh sage
- 1 heaping tablespoon chopped fresh parsley
- ½ cup dry white wine
- 1 cup cream
  Salt and pepper

In large bowl, soak liver slices in milk for 1 hour. Drain and pat dry with paper towels. In 12- to 13-inch skillet, heat butter and quickly cook liver on high heat until firm, but still pink in center. Do not overcook. Remove to warm platter. Stir flour into skillet and add chives, sage, parsley and wine. Stir over low heat and allow to thicken. In small saucepan, heat cream without boiling. Return liver to skillet, stir in warmed cream, add salt and pepper to taste and serve immediately.

Calf's Liver Piccata

1770 HOUSE
East Hampton, New York

6 SERVINGS

LIVER

- 12 slices calf's liver, ¼ inch thick
- ½ cup flour
- ½ teaspoon salt
- ¼ teaspoon pepper
- ¼ cup (½ stick) butter, clarified

PICCATA

- 8 small pitted green olives
- 4 fresh tomatoes, peeled, seeded and slivered
- 3 garlic cloves, crushed
- 1 pimiento, sliced
- ½ cup thinly sliced mushrooms
- 1 tablespoon capers, rinsed and drained
- 4 tablespoons dry white wine
  Parsley, chopped (garnish)

FOR LIVER: Dredge liver slices in flour seasoned with salt and pepper. Shake off excess. Pour butter into 12-inch skillet and sauté liver until it is pink in center, about 3 to 5 minutes on each side. Set aside on serving platter and keep warm.

FOR PICCATA: Into skillet used for liver, place olives, tomatoes, garlic, pimiento, mushrooms and capers. Sauté for several minutes adding more butter if needed and stirring constantly. Push vegetables to one side of skillet, add wine and deglaze pan. Stir vegetables into wine. Return liver slices to pan and heat through. Sprinkle with chopped parsley and serve.

VERSATILE VEAL

When Catherine de Medicis came to France in 1553 to marry the future King Henri II, she brought with her Italian chefs who revolutionized French cuisine. These master cooks contributed to the popularity of veal in Europe through their creation of the many veal dishes that are among the glories of French and Italian cooking.

As a result of improved raising and feeding methods, top-quality veal, while expensive, is now readily available in this country. David Davis, co-innkeeper of Stonehenge and overseer of its superlative kitchen, says veal's popularity is due to the fact that "veal is very versatile, since it is suited to so many sauces and methods of preparation. Veal crosses most international borders of cuisine and is the basis for the national dishes of many countries. Unquestionably, veal may be served in ways to please every palate." Veal recipes in this book include Stonehenge's own creation, Veal Cutlets Gnocchi with Prosciutto Mornay.

Côte de Veau Maintenon

ST. ORRES
Gualala, California

8 SERVINGS

SAUCE SOUBISE
  2 large onions, chopped
  ½ cup (1 stick) butter
  1 cup cooked rice
  ¼ cup whipping cream
  1 tablespoon butter

VEAL
  1 rack of veal, separated into individual chops (8 to rack)
    Salt and pepper
    Oil
  2 cups julienne mushrooms
  2 cups julienne ham
    Butter
  ¾ cup Madeira
  2 tablespoons chopped shallots
  1 cup Demi-glace (see page 175)
    Fresh parsley, finely chopped (garnish)

FOR SAUCE: In 8-inch skillet, cook onions in ½ cup butter over low heat, covered, until soft and lightly golden. Turn off heat and combine cooked rice with onions. Puree in blender or force through sieve. Return puree to skillet. Heat gently, stirring in cream and remaining butter. Turn off heat and cover to keep warm.

FOR VEAL: Preheat oven to 450°F. Season veal with salt and pepper to taste. In 12-inch skillet brown veal quickly in hot oil. Remove to shallow baking dish. Spoon 1 tablespoon of sauce soubise on top of each chop and bake until medium rare, about 17 minutes. In 12-inch skillet, sauté mushrooms and ham in butter. Add ½ cup Madeira and ignite. Add remaining Madeira, shallots and Demi-glace, stirring together well. Place spoonful of soubise sauce on each plate. Place individual chops on soubise. Cover with mushrooms and ham. Sprinkle with parsley and serve immediately.

Medaillons de Veau aux Endives

63

SAN YSIDRO RANCH
Montecito, California

FOR EACH SERVING

SAUCE
  1 teaspoon chopped shallots
  2 teaspoons unsalted butter, room temperature
  2 tablespoons Madeira
    Pinch tarragon
  ¼ cup Brown Sauce (see page 175)
    Salt and pepper to taste

MEAT
  1 veal tenderloin, trimmed clean and sliced into 1-inch medallions
    Salt and pepper
    Flour
  4 tablespoons (½ stick) butter
  1 white or Belgian endive, braised and halved lengthwise (imported canned variety acceptable)
  1 slice pâté de foie, cut in half

FOR SAUCE: In 6-inch skillet, sauté shallots in 1 teaspoon butter until soft but not brown. Add Madeira and tarragon and cook until reduced by two-thirds. Add Brown Sauce, salt and pepper and simmer for 2 minutes. Remove from heat and blend in remaining butter.

FOR MEAT: Season veal medallions with salt and pepper and dredge in flour. In 10-inch skillet, sauté veal in butter, browning both sides until medium done, about 5 to 7 minutes. Do not overcook. Arrange medallions on serving plate and keep warm. Sauté endive briefly in same skillet until heated through and slightly wilted. Cover medallions with pâté slices and top with endive, cut side down. Heat sauce, pour over medallions and serve.

64

Escallopes de Veau Amandine

WINTER'S INN
Kingsfield, Maine

FOR EACH SERVING

    Flour
    Salt and pepper
  2 2-ounce veal cutlets, cut and
    pounded flat
  1 egg, beaten
  ¼ cup finely chopped almonds
  2 tablespoons (¼ stick) butter
    Juice of ½ lemon
    Parsley (garnish)
    Lemon slices (garnish)

In small bowl, combine flour, salt and pepper. Dredge veal in seasoned flour and dip in beaten egg. Press in almonds so both sides are coated. In 10-inch skillet or sauté pan, quickly sauté veal in butter until almonds are golden brown. Turn and squeeze lemon juice over top of veal. Sauté second side until almonds are golden brown. Remove from pan to serving plate. Garnish with parsley and lemon slices. Serve immediately.

Stuffed Veal Andreaux

ARIZONA INN
Tucson, Arizona

4 SERVINGS

    4 strips bacon, diced
    1 large onion, diced
    1 teaspoon minced fresh garlic
    ¼ teaspoon thyme
    6 slices bread, diced
    1 egg
    1 cup veal stock
    1 cup breadcrumbs
      Salt and pepper

    1 pound fresh veal, cut into 4 4-
      ounce slices
    2 tablespoons (¼ stick) butter
  5–6 cups cooked rice, hot
    2 cups Brown Sauce (*see page* 175)

In 10-inch skillet, sauté bacon, onion and garlic until bacon is crisp and onion is golden, about 8 to 10 minutes. Remove from heat and add thyme and bread, mixing well. In large bowl, mix together egg and veal stock. Stir skillet mixture into bowl and mix well. Add sufficient breadcrumbs to bind stuffing. Add salt and pepper to taste.

Pound veal slices to ⅛ inch thick between 2 sheets of waxed paper. Spoon equal amounts of stuffing onto each slice of veal. Roll up and fold ends in, completely enclosing stuffing; secure with toothpick. Add butter to skillet and sauté veal rolls until lightly browned on all sides. Cook over medium heat, uncovered, until veal is tender, about 5 to 8 minutes. Do not overcook as this will toughen veal. Serve on rice with Brown Sauce poured over.

Veal Cutlets Gnocchi

STONEHENGE
Ridgefield, Connecticut

4 SERVINGS

GNOCCHI
  1¼ cups water
   ½ cup (1 stick) butter
   ½ teaspoon salt
  1¼ cups flour
    6 medium eggs
      Dash pepper
      Dash nutmeg
    2 tablespoons grated Gruyère cheese

VEAL
    8 2-ounce veal cutlets, pounded thin
   ½ cup flour
    1 teaspoon salt
   ½ teaspoon pepper
   ¼ cup (½ stick) butter
    1 12-ounce can tomatoes, coarsely
      chopped
    1 ounce thinly sliced prosciutto
   ½ teaspoon garlic powder
   ¼ cup chopped onion
  1½ cups Béchamel Sauce
      (*see page* 175)
   ¾ cup finely grated Gruyère cheese
      Fresh parsley, chopped (garnish)

FOR GNOCCHI: In heavy 6-quart saucepan over medium heat, combine water, butter and salt and bring to boil. Pour in flour all at once and stir vigorously until dough forms ball in center of pan. Remove from heat; allow to cool slightly. Beat in eggs one at a time until mixture is smooth. Season with pepper and nutmeg. Add cheese and beat well. Transfer to bowl. Using same saucepan, rinse and fill ¾ full with

HOMAGE TO ALBERT STOCKLI STONEHENGE

Stonehenge in central Connecticut has a lot to live up to. Its founder was the legendary Albert Stockli, the Swiss-born chef who came to America and, as president of New York's Restaurant Associates, became well known for his adaptations of classic French cuisine and his novel combinations of fresh meats, fish, and vegetables. Mr. Stockli ran the inn for two decades.

These days the converted farmhouse has a mouthwatering list of entrees that would win Mr. Stockli's approval. And the Mocha Tart for dessert has been known to bring conversation to a complete halt.

Veal Manon

Veal Medallions

salted water. Bring to light boil. Fit a pastry bag with plain tip about ¾ inch diameter. Fill bag with gnocchi mixture. Holding bag over boiling water, squeeze out dough in 1-inch lengths, cutting off with knife. Allow gnocchi to tumble freely in boiling water until cooked and tender, about 4 to 5 minutes. Remove with slotted spoon and allow to cool.

FOR VEAL: Preheat oven to 350°F. Dredge cutlets in flour seasoned with salt and pepper. In 12-inch skillet, sauté cutlets in butter over high heat until golden brown on both sides. Cover bottom of 2- to 3-quart casserole with tomatoes. Place cutlets on top of tomatoes and cover with sliced prosciutto. Sprinkle with garlic powder and onion. Arrange gnocchi in casserole and cover contents of casserole with coating of Béchamel Sauce. Sprinkle with cheese. Place casserole in 9 × 13-inch, or large, deep roasting or baking pan. Place pan in oven and pour enough boiling water into pan to reach halfway up exterior of casserole. After water begins to simmer, bake until cheese melts and turns golden brown, about 20 minutes. Sprinkle top with parsley and serve in casserole or on platter.

SAN YSIDRO RANCH
Montecito, California

4 SERVINGS

    2 large artichoke bottoms, cooked
      (*see note page* 29)
 ¾ cup sliced fresh mushrooms
    1 tablespoon chopped shallots
 ¼ cup (½ stick) butter
 ½ tablespoon chopped fresh parsley

    4 6-ounce veal cutlets, cut and
      pounded into scallops
2½ tablespoons vegetable oil, sea-
      soned with salt and pepper to
      taste

Cut each artichoke bottom in half. In 10-inch skillet, sauté artichokes, mushrooms and shallots in butter for 5 minutes. Stir in parsley. Set aside but keep warm.

Preheat broiler. Brush both sides of veal scallops liberally with seasoned oil. Place in shallow broiler pan and broil quickly, about 15 seconds on each side. Transfer to serving platter and top with mushroom and artichoke mixture. Serve immediately.

TOWN FARMS INN
Middletown, Connecticut

2 SERVINGS

SAUCE

    6 tablespoons (¾ stick) butter
    6 fresh mushrooms, sliced
    1 cup light cream
 ½ cup chicken stock
 ¼ cup flour
      Salt and pepper

VEAL

    4 3-ounce veal cutlets
    2 eggs, beaten
      Flour
    4 tablespoons (½ stick) butter
 ¼ cup white wine
    2 teaspoons lemon juice

FOR SAUCE: In 10-inch skillet, melt 2 tablespoons butter and sauté mushrooms. Add cream and chicken stock and bring to boil. Reduce to simmer. In 2-cup saucepan, make roux with ¼ cup butter and flour. Whisk roux into mushroom mixture and cook till thickened. Season to taste with salt and pepper, whisking to smooth sauce.

FOR VEAL: Pound veal to ⅛-inch thickness between 2 sheets of waxed paper. Dip cutlets in beaten eggs and then flour. In 10-inch skillet, sauté cutlets in butter, browning nicely on both sides and cook until tender. Add wine and lemon juice. Pour sauce over cutlets and simmer until very hot, about 3 minutes. Serve immediately.

In 1969, Mark Kaplan was studying to be a doctor and paying for his education by cooking. Eventually, he realized that his true vocation was in the kitchen, so he hung up his forceps for cooking shears. Mark, who has also studied cooking in Europe, constantly refers to approximately 500 cookbooks for new ideas. As he puts it, "One can never know too much, for the art of cooking is always changing and developing." Meanwhile, he has won several first-place honors in American Culinary Federation competitions.

Cuisine at the Pump House, a small inn in Canadensis, Pennsylvania, is so highly regarded that many people who have prepaid meals at nearby hotels dine at the Pump House instead.

DINNER

66 Ham, Chicken and Oysters Yorktown

GOLDEN PHEASANT INN
Erwinna, Pennsylvania

6 SERVINGS

    3 12-ounce whole chicken breasts, boned (or 6 boned halves)
      Flour
      Salt and pepper
½–¾ cup peanut oil
  ¾ cup oyster juice, from shucked oysters
    1 cup heavy cream
    6 thin slices Smithfield (or smoked) ham, trimmed to fit breasts
   18 large fresh oysters, shucked
 1½ cups freshly grated Swiss cheese
    1 tablespoon finely chopped parsley

Skin chicken breasts, halve them if necessary, and pound thin between layers of waxed paper. Dust breasts with flour, salt and pepper. Sauté in hot peanut oil until golden, then transfer to 11 × 7-inch, 2-quart baking dish. Combine oyster juice with cream and pour over chicken breasts. Place 1 slice ham on each breast and 3 oysters on each slice of ham. Sprinkle with cheese and parsley. Bake in a 350°F oven until brown and bubbly, about 30 minutes.

Sweet and Sour Pork

BEEKMAN ARMS
Rhinebeck, New York

8 SERVINGS

 1½ pounds lean pork, cut in 1-inch cubes
 1½ cups flour
    3 tablespoons vegetable oil
 2½ pounds fresh tomatoes, peeled, or 2 16-ounce cans peeled tomatoes
    1 cup dark brown sugar
  ½ cup white vinegar
  ½ cup dark molasses
    3 large green peppers, sliced, room temperature
    1 20-ounce can pineapple chunks or 1 fresh pineapple, cut in chunks, room temperature
    1 teaspoon salt
  ½ teaspoon freshly ground pepper
    1 tablespoon cornstarch dissolved in 2 tablespoons water (optional)
      Rice O'Brien*

Dredge pork in flour. Heat oil in Dutch oven and brown pork lightly. Add tomatoes, sugar, vinegar, molasses and bring to boil. Cook on low heat until pork is tender, about 30 to 40 minutes. Add green peppers, pineapple, salt and pepper. Continue cooking until heated. If desired, add dissolved cornstarch to pork mixture to thicken. Serve with Rice O'Brien.

*Rice O'Brien

8 SERVINGS

8–10 cups cooked rice, hot
   ¼ cup diced red bell pepper
   ¼ cup diced green bell pepper
    3 tablespoons (⅜ stick) butter

Toss rice with butter and diced peppers. Turn rice onto serving platter, spoon pork and sauce over rice and serve immediately.

AN HERB BOUQUET

Chef Mark Kaplan of Pennsylvania's Pump House Inn always keeps an herb mixture on hand for adding zest to meals. The mixture, which can be stored in a tightly sealed glass jar, consists of equal portions of leaf savory, rosemary, thyme, oregano, basil and marjoram. Mark's recipe for Rack of Lamb, below, is a good example of how he uses the mixture to give both flavor and aroma.

Loin of Pork

LOGAN INN
New Hope, Pennsylvania

6 GENEROUS SERVINGS

This dish is as delicious served cold as it is hot.

- 24 small prunes, pitted
  Port wine and hot water to cover prunes (approximately ½ cup each)
  Grated zest of 1 orange
- ½ teaspoon grated ginger root or ¼ teaspoon powdered ginger
- ½ cup coarsely chopped walnut pieces
- 1 4–5-pound pork loin, boned
  Salt and pepper to taste

Place prunes in bowl and cover with mixture of port wine and hot water. Let prunes plump for 1 hour. Drain thoroughly, reserving liquid for basting. Sprinkle prunes with orange zest, ginger and walnuts, turning them with a spoon to cover evenly.

With a sharp knife, cut pocket lengthwise in pork loin approximately ⅔ depth of meat. Spoon prunes into cavity in a tight row. Tie meat at 1½- to 2-inch intervals and close ends with skewers. Salt and pepper meat.

Brown meat lightly on all sides in heavy sauté pan, casserole or Dutch oven. Add a little prune and wine juice for moisture, cover and cook over moderately low heat until thoroughly cooked, about 1½ to 2 hours. Turn meat to cook evenly and baste with prune and wine juices. Serve with strained pan juices thickened with a little cornstarch if desired.

Rack of Lamb

PUMP HOUSE INN
Canadensis, Pennsylvania

2 SERVINGS

Serve with grilled tomato halves sprinkled with Herbed Breadcrumbs.

- 1 rack of baby New Zealand lamb, trimmed of fat with bones Frenched (fat and sinews removed from bones)
- 2 teaspoons mixed herbs (equal amounts leaf savory, rosemary, thyme, oregano, basil, marjoram)
- ¼ teaspoon salt
- 2 turns of black-pepper mill
- 2 pinches garlic powder
- 1 teaspoon imported Dijon mustard

  Herbed Breadcrumbs*

Preheat oven to 450°F. Place lamb fat side down in shallow roasting pan. Sprinkle with herbs, salt, pepper and garlic powder. Bake for 15 minutes and remove from oven. Pour out lamb fat and invert lamb. Spread with mustard and pat on Herbed Breadcrumbs. Return to oven and bake 2 minutes for rare, 4 minutes for medium rare, 6 minutes for medium and 10 minutes for well done.

*Herbed Breadcrumbs

2 SERVINGS

- ½ teaspoon very warm clarified butter
- 1½ teaspoons fine dry breadcrumbs
  Pinch leaf thyme
  Pinch leaf basil
- ½ teaspoon chopped fresh parsley

Spoon butter into warm small bowl. Sprinkle in breadcrumbs and mix well with fork until all crumbs are buttered. Sprinkle in thyme and basil, add parsley and mix thoroughly until herbs are well distributed through buttered crumbs.

WHY NOT RABBIT?

Rabbit has never been in wide demand in this country. Robert Casey, chef at the Town Farms Inn in Connecticut, thinks that's due mostly to lack of publicity. "Rabbit has never been given the extensive promotion that chicken has," he says. "That's too bad because rabbit is readily available frozen, it's all light meat and can be prepared in most of the same ways as chicken."

70 Roast Leg of Lamb

WHEATLEIGH
Lenox, Massachusetts

8 TO 10 SERVINGS

- 1 5–6-pound leg of lamb, trimmed of fat
- 3 cloves garlic, cut thin julienne
  Dried rosemary
- ½ cup cold water
- ½ cup dry red wine
- 1–2 tablespoons tamari* or to taste
  Bunch fresh mint or parsley (garnish)
  Mint jelly (garnish)

Preheat oven to 500°F. Wipe roast with damp cloth. Slash skin in a dozen places and insert strips of fresh garlic. Sprinkle top of lamb with dried rosemary. Put lamb in shallow roasting pan and pour in cold water. Sear lamb in oven until well browned on all sides. Reduce oven to 350°F and continue roasting until meat reaches desired doneness, about 18 minutes per pound for medium rare.

Remove roast to warm platter. Let stand 5 minutes before slicing. Remove as much fat as possible from pan. Pour red wine and tamari into roasting pan. Place over low heat on top of stove. Stir up lamb bits from bottom of pan to include in sauce; cook until slightly reduced. Pour sauce over thinly sliced meat. Garnish with sprigs of mint or parsley and serve with mint jelly.

* A low-salt soy sauce available at natural food stores.

Marinated Leg of Lamb

SIGN OF THE SORREL HORSE
Quakertown, Pennsylvania

6 TO 8 SERVINGS

- 1 5–6-pound butterflied leg of lamb, boned, trimmed of fat and laid flat

SEASONING
- ½ cup finely chopped parsley
- 1 teaspoon salt
- 1 garlic clove, minced
- 1 teaspoon ground rosemary
- ½ teaspoon black pepper
- 1 teaspoon ground ginger
- 1 tablespoon minced shallot or green onion

MARINADE
- ¼ cup Dijon mustard
- 2 tablespoons soy sauce
- 1 tablespoon olive oil
- 1 teaspoon ground rosemary
- 1 teaspoon ground ginger
- 1 garlic clove, minced

FOR SEASONING: In small bowl, combine all ingredients and sprinkle evenly over inside of lamb. Roll and tie.

FOR MARINADE: In same bowl used for seasoning, whisk together all ingredients. Brush entire surface of tied lamb evenly with mixture. Place lamb in shallow roasting pan and cover tightly with plastic wrap. Place in refrigerator several hours or overnight.

Bring meat to room temperature. Preheat oven to 350°F. Roast uncovered for about 1½ hours for medium rare. Let rest before serving with a homemade fruit chutney.

Barbecued Marinated Lamb

FLYING CLOUD INN
New Marlboro, Massachusetts

8 TO 10 SERVINGS

- 1 6-pound butterflied leg of lamb, boned, trimmed of fat, and laid flat
- 1 cup white wine
- 3 tablespoons salad oil
- 2 tablespoons soy sauce
  Juice of 1 lemon
- 2 garlic cloves, crushed
- 1 teaspoon salt
- 1 teaspoon freshly ground pepper
- ½ teaspoon powdered ginger
- 1 bay leaf, crumbled
- ½ teaspoon thyme
- ½ teaspoon sage
- ½ teaspoon marjoram

Place lamb in 13 × 9-inch pan. In bowl, combine all remaining ingredients. Pour over lamb and marinate for at least 3 hours at room temperature. Turn lamb at least once while marinating.

Preheat broiler. Broil on each side until meat is medium rare, about 20 minutes each side. In a saucepan, warm marinade over low heat during last 20 minutes. To serve, slice lamb on diagonal, across the grain. Pour heated marinade over each serving.

First marinated in a well-seasoned stock, rabbit can be turned into a variety of delicious stews. "Town Farms is one of the few inns in New England where rabbit is regularly served," adds Mr. Casey. His recipe for Rabbit Casserole is in this book, as is the Lyme Inn's Hasenpfeffer and a delectable Pâté de Lapin from the Chanticleer Inn.

Lamb Shanks Christina

CHALET SUZANNE
Lake Wales, Florida

4 SERVINGS

    4 slices bacon, diced
    4 lamb shanks
      Salt and pepper to taste
      Flour
    1 16-ounce can tomatoes
    1 cup chopped celery
    1 cup dry red Burgundy
    ½ cup chopped parsley
    2 medium onions, sliced
    1 tablespoon grated horseradish,
      fresh or bottled
    1 garlic clove, minced
    1 teaspoon Worcestershire sauce
    ½ pound fresh mushrooms, sliced
    1 tablespoon cornstarch, dissolved
      in 3 tablespoons water (optional)

In large skillet, cook bacon slowly over low heat to render fat. Remove bacon bits and reserve both fat and bacon. Season shanks well with salt and pepper and dredge in flour. Brown shanks slowly in reserved bacon fat for 15 to 20 minutes, turning to brown evenly. Add tomatoes, bacon bits, celery, wine, parsley, onions, horseradish, garlic and Worcestershire sauce. Cover and simmer until shanks are tender, about 2½ hours. Add mushrooms and cook 5 minutes. If desired, thicken gravy with dissolved cornstarch.

Hasenpfeffer

LYME INN
Lyme, New Jersey

6 TO 8 SERVINGS

    2 cups red wine
    1 cup vinegar
    1 cup water
    1 tablespoon lemon juice
    5 garlic cloves, chopped
   12 peppercorns
    2 celery stalks, minced
    ¼ teaspoon marjoram
    ¼ teaspoon thyme
    2 3-pound rabbits, cut in pieces

    2 tablespoons (¼ stick) butter
    8 slices bacon, diced
    1 onion, diced
    ½ cup sliced mushrooms
    ½ cup flour seasoned with salt and
      pepper
    ¼ cup sour cream

In large shallow pan, combine wine, vinegar, water, lemon juice, garlic, peppercorns, celery, marjoram and thyme. Add rabbit and marinate for 2 days.

Remove rabbit from marinade; reserve marinade. In Dutch oven, melt butter and sauté bacon, onion and mushrooms until bacon is crispy and onion is tender. Dredge rabbit pieces in seasoned flour and sauté in Dutch oven until browned evenly. Strain reserved marinade and pour over rabbit pieces in Dutch oven. Cover and simmer until rabbit is tender, about 45 minutes. Remove from heat and blend in sour cream. Serve immediately.

Rabbit Casserole

TOWN FARMS INN
Middletown, Connecticut

3 SERVINGS

    1 3-pound rabbit, cut in
      6–8 pieces
      Flour
      Olive oil
    1 cup chicken stock
    1 cup dry white wine
    1 cup red Burgundy
    2 stalks celery, chopped
    1 large onion, diced
    1 carrot, sliced
    ⅛ teaspoon poultry seasoning
      Pinch salt
      Pinch pepper
    1 tablespoon cornstarch, dissolved
      in 2 tablespoons water
    6 mushrooms, quartered

Preheat oven to 350°F. Dredge rabbit pieces in flour. In 10-inch skillet, sauté rabbit in oil until evenly browned. In shallow roasting pan or Dutch oven, combine chicken stock, white and red wines, celery, onion, carrot, poultry seasoning, salt and pepper. Add rabbit, cover and bake until almost done, about 60 minutes. Remove rabbit to platter and thicken sauce with dissolved cornstarch. Adjust seasoning to taste and strain. Place rabbit and mushrooms in earthenware casserole, pour sauce over and bake, covered, until rabbit is tender, about 20 minutes.

72 Baked Breast of Chicken

EXCELSIOR HOUSE
Jefferson, Texas

4 TO 6 SERVINGS

  6 8-ounce chicken breast halves, boned and skinned
     Garlic salt
  ½ cup (1 stick) butter or margarine, melted
  1 teaspoon paprika
  3 tablespoons lemon juice
  1 cup sour cream, room temperature
  ¼ cup sherry
  2 4-ounce cans mushroom stems and pieces, drained
     Generous dash cayenne pepper

Preheat oven to 375°F. Sprinkle chicken with garlic salt to taste. Mix together margarine or butter, paprika and lemon juice. Brush chicken breasts well with butter mixture and place in shallow baking pan. Bake under foil tent until tender, about 30 minutes, brushing occasionally with remaining butter mixture to keep from drying. In a bowl, blend together sour cream, sherry, mushrooms and cayenne pepper. Pour mixture over chicken for last 15 minutes of baking.

Chicken in Phyllo

WINDFLOWER INN
Great Barrington, Massachusetts

8 SERVINGS

  4 whole chicken breasts, halved and boned
  4 cups chicken stock
  1 cup Chablis
  2 celery stalks, minced
  2 carrots, minced
  1 onion, minced
  6 sprigs parsley, minced
     Salt and freshly ground pepper to taste
  6 tablespoons (¾ stick) butter
  3 tablespoons flour
  8 sheets phyllo dough (may be purchased ready-made)

In 9½-inch, 3½-quart sauté pan, place chicken breasts, chicken stock and Chablis. Add vegetables, parsley, salt and pepper. Cover and cook over medium heat at slow simmer until chicken is tender, about 15 minutes. Remove chicken breasts; set aside to cool. Reduce stock to about 2 cups. Place vegetables and stock in blender or food processor and puree. Pour puree into top half of double boiler and keep hot, not allowing sauce to boil.

In 1-cup saucepan, melt 3 tablespoons butter, blend in flour and cook over medium heat for 2 minutes, stirring constantly to make roux. Add roux to heated puree, whisking until smooth. Place top half of double boiler on direct heat and bring contents to slow boil, stirring over medium heat until sauce has thickened, about 2 minutes. Return pan to double boiler and keep sauce very warm.

Preheat oven to 350°F. Place each chicken breast at one end of phyllo sheet crosswise to length of phyllo. Top each breast with 1 teaspoon sauce. Fold sides of phyllo inward to partially cover chicken. Roll chicken in phyllo the entire length of sheet. Brush tops with remaining melted butter and place on greased baking sheet. Bake until phyllo is nicely browned, about 15 minutes, then brush with melted butter and bake for additional 15 minutes. Serve with warm sauce.

NOTE: If desired, after wrapping chicken in phyllo and brushing generously with butter, you may refrigerate or freeze this dish. (Freeze sauce separately.) Bake directly from freezer for an additional 15 to 20 minutes.

AT THE SIGN OF THE SORREL HORSE

Lost in the middle of eastern Pennsylvania, the Sign of the Sorrel Horse is an eighteenth-century tavern that has become headquarters for a very sophisticated food operation. Running the show are three people in their early thirties: Fred Cresson and chefs Ron Strouse and Hannah Robinson, graduates of Philadelphia's Restaurant School.

Their philosophy: "To challenge our guests to try something different, and to offer a menu that strikes a balance between being mundane and off the wall." The inn is in Quakertown, about a half-hour drive outside Philadelphia, but judging from the long reservations list, the food is well worth the trip.

Chicken Oriental

SAXTONS RIVER INN
Saxtons River, Vermont

8 SERVINGS

    8 chicken breasts, boned, split and
      skinned
    2 tablespoons tamari
    ½ cup (1 stick) butter, melted
    2 carrots, coarsely chopped
    1 small head broccoli, coarsely
      chopped
    1 small head cauliflower, coarsely
      chopped
    1 medium eggplant, coarsely
      chopped
    1 green pepper, coarsely chopped
    4 green onions, coarsely chopped
   12 small mushrooms, sliced
   16 cherry tomatoes
    2 tablespoons finely chopped fresh
      parsley
    ½ cup sliced almonds
      Dash pepper

      Parslied Rice*

Cut breasts into long, thin slices. Place in bowl, sprinkle with tamari and stir well. Pour ¼ cup butter into 10-inch skillet over low heat. Pour remaining butter into 11-inch sauté pan. Cook chicken in skillet, stirring occasionally until lightly golden, about 3 to 5 minutes. Put vegetables, except mushrooms and tomatoes, into sauté pan. Cook over high heat for 4 to 5 minutes, turning occasionally. They should still be crisp. Reduce heat to medium. Add mushrooms and tomatoes. Continue to cook about 2 more minutes. Add chicken, parsley and almonds. Season with pepper and mix well. Cover and continue cooking until flavors are mingled, about 1 minute. Serve on plates over Parslied Rice.

*Parslied Rice

MAKES 8 SERVINGS

    2 cups rice
   2½ tablespoons olive oil
    2 tablespoons chopped parsley
    5 cups cold water

In 2-quart heavy saucepan or sauté pan, heat rice and parsley in olive oil until golden brown. Add water, bring to boil. Stir once with fork and reduce to simmer. Cook covered until water is absorbed, about 15 to 20 minutes.

Lemon Walnut Chicken

1770 HOUSE
East Hampton, New York

6 SERVINGS

CHICKEN

    3 whole chicken breasts
      Salt and pepper to taste
    ½ cup (1 stick) butter
    ½ cup oil
      Flour
   1-2 eggs, beaten

SAUCE

    ¼ cup (½ stick) butter
    1 teaspoon minced garlic
    1 teaspoon minced shallot
    1 tablespoon flour
   1½ cups chicken stock
    ½ cup dry Marsala
      Juice of 1 lemon or to taste

    ½ cup chopped walnuts, toasted
      (garnish)
      Fresh parsley, finely chopped
      (garnish)
    1 whole lemon, thinly sliced
      (garnish)

FOR CHICKEN: Skin and bone chicken breasts and cut in half. Trim well and season with salt and pepper. (Trimmings may be used to make stock for sauce.) Heat butter and oil together in 12-inch skillet. Dredge each chicken piece in flour and shake off excess. Dip chicken in beaten eggs and sauté in hot fat until golden on both sides. Drain on paper towels.

FOR SAUCE: Melt butter in 1-quart saucepan. Add garlic and shallot and sauté for a minute. Add flour, stirring constantly. Do not allow mixture to brown. Add stock and Marsala and

Suprême de Volaille

PUMP HOUSE INN
Canadensis, Pennsylvania

continue to stir until smooth and slightly thickened. Add lemon juice.

Preheat oven to 375°F. Place drained chicken pieces in fancy shallow baking dish or gratin pan. Pour sauce over chicken and bake until chicken is tender, about 20 to 30 minutes. When ready to serve, sprinkle with chopped walnuts, parsley and fresh lemon slices.

FOR EACH SERVING

STUFFING
- 2 tablespoons (¼ stick) clarified butter
- 2 tablespoons diced onion
- 2 teaspoons diced celery
- 1 teaspoon diced green pepper
- 1 medium mushroom, diced
- ½ medium pork sausage, cubed
- ⅓ teaspoon garlic powder
- 3 tablespoons dry white wine
- 2 pinches mixed herbs (equal parts leaf thyme, oregano, basil)
- 2 roasted and shelled chestnuts, halved
- ⅓ cup whipping cream
- 1 slice stale bread, cubed
  Salt and freshly ground pepper to taste

CHICKEN
- ½ pound boneless whole chicken breast, skinned and pounded between waxed paper to flatten
  Flour
- 6 tablespoons (¾ stick) clarified butter
- ¾ cup rich chicken or veal stock
- ½ small garlic clove, crushed
- ½ teaspoon chopped parsley
- 3 mushrooms, quartered
- 1 teaspoon diced shallots
- ¼ cup dry sherry

FOR STUFFING: Heat butter in heavy skillet and add onions, celery, green pepper and mushroom. Cook vegetables over medium flame for 5 minutes; then add sausage, garlic powder, white wine, herbs and chestnuts. Cook until wine has reduced, about 10 minutes. Add cream and bread. Cook until cream is absorbed, about 5 minutes, then add salt and pepper. (Add 3 more tablespoons cream for a richer texture, if desired.) Use warm stuffing immediately or refrigerate until chilled.

FOR CHICKEN: Preheat oven to 400°F. Place stuffing on chicken breast and fold to encase stuffing. Fasten with small skewers or picks. Dust chicken breast lightly with flour and sauté in remaining butter in a large ovenproof skillet or shallow casserole until lightly browned, about 4 minutes per side. While chicken is cooking, bring stock to boil in 2-cup saucepan. Add garlic, parsley, mushrooms, shallots and sherry to chicken and cook over medium heat for 1 minute. Pour in stock and bake covered in oven for 15 minutes.

Remove skewers, slice breast into 6 pieces and serve immediately, covered with sauce.

On New Year's Eve The Elms rolls out the wild boar along with the party horns. Later in the year the celebration is for Morels, those wonderfully flavorful mushrooms, but no matter what the occasion, The Elms is the place to celebrate. A family-run operation with a superb menu and wine list, The Elms is a 200-year-old inn that is tucked away in the southern Connecticut village of Ridgefield.

Chicken Luau

Chicken Ridgefield

CHALET SUZANNE
Lake Wales, Florida

10 TO 12 SERVINGS

Prepare 24 hours in advance for best flavor.

- 3 3–4-pound frying chickens, disjointed and skinned
  Flour
  Salt and pepper
- ¼ cup peanut oil

- 1½ cups (3 sticks) butter
- 3 large onions, chopped fine
- 3 cups minced parsley
- 2 or 3 garlic cloves, crushed
- 3 large green peppers, finely chopped
- 3 1-pound 13-ounce cans tomatoes
- 2 tablespoons vinegar
- 2 tablespoons mustard
- 1 tablespoon each: salt, pepper, curry powder, thyme
- 3 cups currants
- 2 cups slivered almonds

Dredge chicken in flour seasoned with salt and pepper. In extra large skillet, heat oil. Fry chicken until tender, 20 to 25 minutes, turning to brown evenly. Remove from pan, cool, and refrigerate for 24 hours.

Preheat oven to 350°F. Place chicken in large roasting pan and cover with foil. Bake until heated. In 12-inch skillet, melt butter and sauté onions, parsley and garlic until onions are limp but not browned, 8 to 10 minutes. Add peppers, tomatoes, vinegar, mustard, salt, pepper, curry and thyme and simmer for 30 minutes. Add currants and almonds. Heat, pour over chicken and serve.

THE ELMS
Ridgefield, Connecticut

4 TO 6 SERVINGS

CHICKEN
- 1 2½-pound chicken, boned
  Flour
  Salt and pepper to taste
- ½ cup (1 stick) butter (as needed)
- 4 tablespoons white wine
- 4 medium mushrooms, diced
- 2 shallots, finely chopped
- 4 tablespoons Brown Sauce (see page 175)

PASTRY SHELL
- ½ cup plus 2 tablespoons flour
- 1 egg
- ½ cup milk
  Oil

FOR CHICKEN: Dredge chicken in flour seasoned with salt and pepper. In 12-inch skillet, sauté chicken in butter until golden brown on all sides. Add wine, shallots, mushrooms and Brown Sauce and simmer slowly, uncovered, until chicken is tender, about 20 minutes.

FOR PASTRY SHELL: Preheat oven to 475°F. In medium bowl, beat together flour, egg and milk to form a heavy batter thick enough to coat spoon like heavy cream. Take two steel or other heavy all-metal omelet or crepe pans with sharply sloping or rounded sides; one about 6-inch diameter at bottom and 8½-inch diameter at top, the other small enough to fit inside. Make sure underneath of smaller pan is clean. Brush bottom and sides of larger pan with oil and heat both pans very hot. Spoon and swirl enough batter into large pan to cover bottom and sides ⅛ inch thick. To mold the shell, place the smaller pan over top of crepe mixture. When shell is molded, place larger pan in oven and bake until crepe is set, cooked through and browned on top and bottom, about 5 to 7 minutes. Remove from oven, strike bottom of pan on stove burner to loosen crepe and slip crepe into large bowl to support raised sides. Repeat until all batter is used. When ready to use, slip layered crepe shell out of bowl and place on baking sheet or in large shallow roasting pan. Arrange chicken in shell and bake until shell is hot and crusty, about 2 to 4 minutes.

JARRED CHICKEN
A prize winner

Mrs. Elbert Hubbard II won a prize for Jarred Chicken in a "Fit for a Queen Recipe" contest sponsored in the 1930s by the *Buffalo Courier-Express*. Mrs. Hubbard was the daughter-in-law of Elbert Hubbard, noted author and founder of Roycroft Industries, whose East Aurora home is now the Roycroft Inn. Her recipe is still served at the inn.

76 Smothered Chicken

WAYSIDE INN
Middletown, Virginia

2 SERVINGS

- 1 1½–2-pound chicken, halved
- 1 tablespoon butter
- 1 cup dry white wine
  Salt and pepper to taste
- 1 cup chicken consommé

Preheat oven to 350°F. Put chicken in shallow 10×6-inch baking pan skin side up and dot with butter. Bake uncovered for 15 minutes, turning once to lightly brown both sides. Add wine, salt and pepper. Cover and steam in oven for 15 minutes. Remove cover and continue to bake until leg yields readily to pressure and chicken is tender, about 10 to 15 minutes, turning occasionally to brown. Allow all liquid to cook away and crisp chicken. Remove to heated platter. Add consommé to baking pan. Cook mixture until slightly thickened, scraping pan to loosen browned particles. Serve over chicken.

Jarred Chicken

ROYCROFT INN
East Aurora, New York

4 TO 6 SERVINGS

- 1 cup flour
- 3 teaspoons salt
- 1 teaspoon freshly ground pepper
- ½ teaspoon paprika
- 1 6-pound chicken, cut into serving pieces
- 2 tablespoons (¼ stick) butter
- 2 tablespoons rendered chicken fat or other shortening
  Half and half
  Milk
- ½ pound mushrooms, sliced

In medium to large brown paper bag, combine flour, salt, pepper and paprika. Place chicken in bag. Close tightly and shake well to coat chicken with flour mixture. Place bag in refrigerator and chill for 1 hour. Before frying be sure each piece is well coated with flour.

Preheat oven to 300°F. In 12-inch heavy skillet over medium to high heat, combine butter with chicken fat or shortening and quickly sauté chicken on all sides until golden brown. Add more butter if needed to brown all pieces. Put chicken in 2-quart casserole and pour sufficient equal parts half and half and milk to cover chicken. Cover with tight-fitting lid or foil and bake for 1 hour. Remove from oven and add mushrooms, pushing slices down between pieces of chicken. If necessary, add more milk. Cover and bake until chicken is tender, about 30 minutes.

Turkey Breast Ambassador

ARIZONA INN
Tucson, Arizona

4 SERVINGS

- 1 pound fresh raw turkey breast, boned and cut in 4-ounce slices (or packaged raw turkey breast slices)
  Salt and white pepper to taste
- ¼ cup (½ stick) butter or oil
- 1 cup flour
- 4 eggs, beaten
- 1 avocado, peeled and sliced
- 1 tomato, sliced
- ½ pound mozzarella cheese, sliced

Pound turkey slices ⅛ inch thick between 2 sheets waxed paper. Season lightly with salt and pepper. In large skillet, heat butter or oil. Dip turkey in flour, then in egg wash. Sauté over medium-high heat, turning to prevent burning, until golden brown on both sides. Remove to broiler pan.

Preheat broiler. Arrange avocado and tomato slices on top of each slice of turkey. Top with cheese slices. Broil until cheese melts, about 3 to 5 minutes.

RIGHT:
Grilled Red Snapper
from the Inn at Sawmill Farm,
West Dover, Vermont.
See page 87.

Mountain Trout Amandine from the Red Fox Tavern, Middleburg, Virginia. *See page* 89.

LEFT:
Coquilles St. Jacques
as it is served at
St. Orres Inn,
Gualala, California.
See note, pages 32–33.

RIGHT:
Shrimp Scampi
from The Victorian,
Whitinsville,
Massachusetts.
See page 92.

A SPECIAL WAY OF COOKING TROUT

Brook Trout "en bleu" is a dramatic speciality of Connecticut's Stonehenge and its flavor is said to be unmatched. The trout is kept alive in a tank until the last minute before being poached in a court bouillon laced with vinegar, which turns the fish blue. It is then skinned and boned at the table and served with a mousseline sauce.

A SPECIAL WAY TO COOK SALMON

Chef Franz Buck of Salishan Lodge holding a Potlach salmon barbecued for banquets following the method used by Salish Indians of the Northwest coast. A large 24-pound fillet of Chinook salmon is secured and cooked upright against a cone of hot coals for 1 hour. An alder board and sticks can also be used to strap in the fillet. After tasting Chinook salmon cooked this way, guests know why it is also called "King."

OVERLEAF:
Ingredients for
Famous Vegetable Chowder
from The Homestead,
Sugar Hill, New Hampshire.
See page 97.

Kedron Valley in South Woodstock, Vermont is an old-time New England inn complete with its own maple sugar factory and a large horse stable. In winter, guests are treated to a ride on the inn's horse-drawn sleigh. Meanwhile in the kitchen, Mrs. Beatrix Kendall, 77-year-old mother of the owners, is busy making desserts to warm the returning travelers.

DINNER

Quail with Grapes and Cognac

SIGN OF THE SORREL HORSE
Quakertown, Pennsylvania

4 SERVINGS

- 8 quail
  Salt and pepper
- ¼ cup (½ stick) butter, melted
- 4 slices bacon, halved
- ½ cup beef stock or canned beef bouillon
- 20 (approximately) white fresh or canned seedless grapes, peeled
- ¼ cup Cognac
- 2 tablespoons (¼ stick) butter

Preheat oven to 400°F. Rinse quail and pat dry. Trim neck and discard giblets. Truss legs tightly to body with string or butcher's twine. Season lightly with salt and pepper and coat with melted butter. Place in shallow roasting pan, breasts up. Place ½ slice bacon lengthwise over each quail to keep breasts moist. Roast until tender, about 15 to 18 minutes. Transfer quail to heated platter and remove butcher's twine and bacon. Pour beef stock and Cognac into roasting pan and cook over high heat until reduced to two-thirds cup. Add grapes and simmer over medium heat to poach them lightly. Remove from heat, stir in remaining butter and spoon over quail.

LEFT:
Lobster Bisque
from the Copper Beech Inn,
Ivoryton, Connecticut.
See page 110.

Baked Fish, Sauce Dubrovnik

THE ELMS
Ridgefield, Connecticut

6 SERVINGS

- 2 tablespoons (¼ stick) butter
- 2 tablespoons flour
- 1 garlic clove, crushed
- 2 teaspoons white wine vinegar
- 4 tablespoons dry white wine
- 6 1-inch-thick fish steaks (any firm fresh fish, free of bones)
- 1 16-ounce can crushed tomatoes

Preheat oven to 425°F. Lightly butter bottom of 13 × 9-inch shallow baking pan; set aside. In small saucepan over low heat, melt butter and add flour to make roux. Add garlic, vinegar and wine, blending well with roux. Cook on medium heat, whisking occasionally, until blended and slightly thickened, about 5 minutes. Remove from heat. Place fish steaks in baking pan and cover with wine mixture. Pour crushed tomatoes over top. Bake until fish flakes easily without being dry, about 10 minutes.

Fillets of Sole Cornelius

85

KEDRON VALLEY INN
South Woodstock, Vermont

4 SERVINGS

- 1 ounce finely chopped shallots
- 2 pounds fillet of sole
  Salt and ground red pepper
- 1 lobster tail cut into ¼-inch-thick slices (crabmeat or shrimp may be substituted)
- 1 cup Riesling (or other semi-dry wine)
- 3 cups fish Velouté (*see page 176*)
- 1 ounce diced truffles or 4 black pitted olives, diced
- 3 tablespoons whipping cream
- 2 tablespoons (¼ stick) butter, room temperature, cut in small pieces

Preheat oven to 400°F. Sprinkle shallots evenly over inside of shallow 10 × 6-inch baking pan. Season fillets with salt and red pepper and arrange over shallots. Top with lobster slices. Pour wine over fish and cover with sheet of buttered waxed paper. Bring to boil over direct heat. Transfer to oven and bake until fish flakes easily, about 25 minutes.

While fish bakes, warm fish Velouté in heavy saucepan over low heat. When fish is done, pour liquid into small saucepan; cover fish lightly and keep warm. Cook liquid over medium heat until reduced by half. Strain into Velouté. Add truffles or olives and cream and bring to a rolling boil. Remove sauce from heat and whisk in butter a piece at a time, stirring until each piece has melted before adding more. Adjust seasoning. Pour sauce over fish and serve immediately.

86 Flounder with Mussels and Clams

THE 1661 INN
Block Island, Rhode Island

6 TO 10 SERVINGS

TOMATO SAUCE

 1 garlic clove, minced
 2 tablespoons (¼ stick) butter
 ⅔ cup minced onion
 ¼ cup minced celery
 ⅓ cup flour
 2½ cups brown stock or beef broth, heated
 1½ cups tomato puree
 ¾ cup peeled, seeded and chopped tomatoes
 1 bay leaf
 ½ teaspoon dried thyme
 ½ teaspoon freshly ground pepper
 1 whole clove
   Salt

MUSSELS AND CLAMS

 ¼ cup minced onion
 2 teaspoons butter
 ⅓ cup sliced pitted black olives
 ¼ cup minced mushrooms
 ⅛ teaspoon dried summer savory
 ¼ cup dry white wine
 ½ cup whole mussels
 ½ cup chopped clams
   Salt and freshly ground pepper

FLOUNDER

 12 flounder fillets
   Salt and pepper

FOR TOMATO SAUCE: In 3-quart heavy saucepan, sauté garlic in butter until golden. Add onion and celery and sauté until onion is softened. Add flour and cook over medium-high heat, stirring constantly until roux just begins to change color, about 5 minutes. Remove from heat and gradually add stock or beef broth. Return to heat and stir frequently until sauce is smooth and thickened, about 5 minutes. Add tomato puree, tomatoes, bay leaf, thyme, pepper and clove. Simmer slowly, stirring occasionally, for 1½ hours. Strain through sieve into bowl. Add salt to taste.

FOR MUSSELS AND CLAMS: In large deep skillet, sauté onion in butter until softened. Stir in olives, mushrooms and summer savory. Add 2 cups of tomato sauce. Simmer, covered, stirring occasionally, for five minutes. Add wine and simmer, uncovered, for ten minutes. Add mussels and clams. Season with salt and pepper to taste.

FOR FLOUNDER: Preheat oven to 375°F. Slightly flatten flounder fillets by pounding between two layers of waxed paper. Sprinkle lightly with salt and pepper. Spoon about 2 tablespoons of mussel and clam mixture onto gray side of each fillet. Roll fillets and arrange in 13½ × 8¾-inch baking dish in one layer. Pour remaining mussels and clams over fillets and bake until they flake easily when tested with a fork, about 12 to 15 minutes.

Marinated Ling Cod*

HARBOR HOUSE
Elk, California

6 SERVINGS

   Salt and pepper
 6 6–9-ounce ling cod (or red snapper) fillets
 ¾ cup olive oil
 1 tablespoon mustard
 1 tablespoon red wine vinegar
 1 teaspoon horseradish
 ½ teaspoon paprika
 1 teaspoon garlic juice
   Pinch curry
   Pinch ground red pepper
   Breadcrumbs

Salt and pepper fillets and arrange in 10 × 6-inch baking dish. In a jar, combine remaining ingredients except breadcrumbs. Cover and shake vigorously. Cover fillets with marinade and marinate for 1½ to 2 hours. Lift or turn fillets occasionally so that marinade covers all surfaces thoroughly.

Preheat broiler at least 10 minutes. Remove fillets from marinade, roll in breadcrumbs and arrange them on broiler rack. Sprinkle with some of remaining marinade. Broil 2 inches from flame until each side is light golden brown, about 4 minutes each side.

* A California variety of Pacific bottom fish. Not a true member of cod family.

Brill Williams, chef at the Inn at Sawmill Farm, West Dover, Vermont. His recipe for grilled red snapper appears below.

Poisson Oriental

PILGRIM'S INN
Deer Isle, Maine

Serve with rice or noodles.

4 SERVINGS
MARINADE
3–6 ounces canned orange juice concentrate, thawed
2–4 tablespoons tamari* or other good Japanese soy sauce
½–1 inch ginger root, freshly ground**

FISH
4 8-ounce fish fillets (any white fish such as sole, flounder or cod)
Salt and freshly ground pepper
Garlic powder
Flour or cracker crumbs
6 tablespoons (¾ stick) butter

FOR MARINADE: Mix together orange juice concentrate, soy sauce, and ground ginger.

FOR FISH: Layer fish fillets in 10 × 6-inch glass or ceramic baking dish. Sprinkle lightly with salt, pepper and garlic. Cover with marinade. Marinate fish at least 4 hours.

Preheat oven to 400°F. Remove fish from marinade, permit excess marinade to drip into baking dish, and coat fish lightly with flour or cracker crumbs. In 10-inch skillet, brown lightly in butter on each side. Return to baking dish, cover with marinade and bake in oven until fish flakes easily, about 8 to 10 minutes.

* A low-salt soy sauce available in natural food stores.
** To have freshly ground ginger always available, purchase fresh ginger root and store in freezer. Grate as needed and return remaining ginger to freezer.

Grilled Red Snapper with Fresh Sorrel Sauce

INN AT SAWMILL FARM
West Dover, Vermont

6 TO 8 SERVINGS
SAUCE
8 shallots, finely chopped
¾ cup dry vermouth
¼ cup sherry
2 cups Béchamel Sauce (see page 175)
2 egg yolks, beaten
Juice of 1 lemon
Salt and freshly ground black pepper
Ground red pepper
Nutmeg
8–10 fresh sorrel leaves, chopped

FISH
3½ pounds fillet of red snapper, rock cod or rock fish, in 1 or 2 pieces
Oil or melted butter
Salt and freshly ground black pepper
Blanched almonds, sliced

FOR SAUCE: In 1-quart saucepan, boil shallots in vermouth and sherry until liquid is reduced to ¾ cup, about 10 minutes. Make Béchamel in 4-quart saucepan. When it is smooth and thick, add egg yolks, lemon juice, salt, peppers, and nutmeg, stirring well with whisk. Add shallot mixture and sorrel and stir well. Keep warm.

FOR FISH: Prepare barbecue or preheat broiler very hot for 10 to 15 minutes. Place fish skin side down on platter, brush well with oil or melted butter and sprinkle with salt and pepper. In hinged twin-rack broiler, broil over open fire, or under broiler in well-oiled or foil-lined broiler pan until fish flakes, 10 to 15 minutes. Sprinkle lightly with almonds. Pass sauce separately.

88 Salmon-Stuffed Fillet of Sole

THE VICTORIAN
Whitinsville, Massachusetts

8 TO 10 SERVINGS

STUFFING
- ½ pound cooked salmon, crumbled
- 2 teaspoons lemon juice, or to taste
- 1 3-ounce package cream cheese, unwrapped and room temperature
- 2 eggs
  Pinch dill

SAUCE
- 4 tablespoons (½ stick) butter
- 4 tablespoons flour
- ¾ cup milk
- ¾ cup clam juice
- ⅓–½ cup dry white wine or ⅓ cup heavy cream with 1 tablespoon lemon juice
  Salt and pepper
- 1½ teaspoons fresh tarragon or ¾ teaspoon dried
- 8–10 large or 16–20 small fillets of sole, skinned
- 4 tablespoons grated Swiss cheese

FOR STUFFING: In small bowl, mix salmon, lemon juice, cream cheese, eggs, and dill. Puree in blender or food processor, or use potato masher.

FOR SAUCE: In 1-quart saucepan, melt butter and add flour to make roux. Do not allow to brown. Meanwhile, in 2-cup saucepan, bring milk and clam juice to boil, then add to roux. Sauce should be rather thick. Thin with either white wine or cream and lemon juice mixture, until sauce coats spoon easily. Add salt and pepper to taste and tarragon.

TO ASSEMBLE: Preheat oven to 400°F. On small end of sole place 2 tablespoons of stuffing. Roll up neatly. Allow one large or two small rolls per person. Put ½ cup sauce in bottom of 12×9- or 13×9-inch baking or roasting pan which will hold the fish in one layer. Lay stuffed rolls of fish on top of sauce. Spoon remaining sauce over fish. Bake, uncovered, until fish flakes easily, about 20 minutes, depending on density of fish. Cover with grated cheese; brown under broiler and serve.

Fillet of Sole Marguery

SALISHAN LODGE
Gleneden Beach, Oregon

FOR EACH SERVING

- Butter
- 1 teaspoon minced shallots
- 2 4–5-ounce trimmed fillets of sole, folded or rolled skin side in
  Salt and white pepper
- 1 ounce Oregon or bay shrimp
- 3 mushrooms, quartered or sliced
  Dry white wine
  Fish Stock for Sole*
- ¼ cup Béchemal Sauce (see page 175)
- 2 tablespoons Hollandaise Sauce (see page 176)
- 3 canned or fresh mussels (garnish)
  Parsley (garnish)
  Lemon slices (garnish)

Butter a shallow sauté pan. Sprinkle shallots on bottom of pan and arrange sole on top. Salt and pepper to taste. Distribute shrimp and mushroom in empty spaces between fish. Add equal combination of just enough wine and fish stock to barely cover sole. Bring to quick boil, reduce heat and simmer until sole flakes easily when prodded with fork, about 3 to 4 minutes. Do not overcook. Remove fish with slotted spatula to heated platter and keep warm. Arrange shrimp and mushrooms around or on top of sole. Reduce liquids in sauté pan by two-thirds. Add Béchemal Sauce to liquids in pan to thicken. Strain. Fold Hollandaise Sauce into thickened strained mixture. Adjust seasoning and spoon over sole, shrimp and mushrooms. In small saucepan, heat mussels. Garnish sole with mussels, parsley and lemon slices.

Gene Bellows, the chef and owner of the Bee and Thistle Inn, with a hefty slab of swordfish prior to preparing it for dinner.

Swordfish Chinois Baked in Paper

1770 HOUSE
East Hampton, New York

6 SERVINGS

Parchment paper
6 6–8-ounce slices of swordfish, ½–¾ inch thick (or any firm fish such as tile, halibut, cod)
¼ cup light soy sauce
¼ cup Chinese sesame oil
2 tablespoons sherry
6 scallions, julienned, using 2 inches of the green
1 teaspoon minced garlic
1 teaspoon minced ginger root

Preheat oven to 400°F. Cut 6 heart shapes from the paper, each large enough to encase a piece of fish on half a heart with room to spare. Fold paper in half lengthwise and, on the right side of each heart, place a piece of fish. In bowl, combine remaining ingredients and spoon over fish. Fold paper over fish and twist pointed end together, then fold and crimp halves together to seal package tightly. You may use paper clips. Place packages of fish on a baking sheet and bake in oven about 10 to 15 minutes. Cooking time depends on thickness of fish. Do not overcook. Paper should brown and puff up. Remove to serving dish. Using scissors, cut open, or cut a cross in center and fold back the four points.

Mountain Trout Amandine

RED FOX TAVERN
Middleburg, Virginia

FOR EACH SERVING

1 trout
¼ cup (½ stick) clarified butter
Flour
1 egg, beaten
2 tablespoons slivered blanched almonds
3 tablespoons white wine
Squeeze of fresh lemon juice

Clean and scale trout. If desired, with fillet knife or scissors, remove backbone and rib bones. Wash trout in cold salted water, wipe with damp cloth. In 8- or 10-inch skillet depending on trout size, heat butter until very hot but not smoking. Dust trout with flour, dip in egg wash and sauté immediately over medium heat until each side is nicely golden brown, about 5 minutes on first side and 3 to 5 minutes on second side. Remove trout to serving dish and keep warm. Add almonds to skillet and brown lightly. Add wine and lemon juice. Cook until slightly reduced, scraping pan to loosen browned bits. Pour juices over trout and serve immediately.

*Fish Stock for Sole

MAKES 2 QUARTS

Butter
2 pounds raw fishbones and trimmings, coarsely chopped (sole or whiting bones are best for this stock)
4–6 stalks parsley
1 onion, minced
Pinch salt
Juice from canned mussels (optional)
1 celery stalk (optional)
1 carrot (optional)
1 bay leaf (optional)
1½ quarts water
2 cups dry white wine

Butter 3½- to 4-quart saucepan. Place bones and trimmings, parsley, onion and salt in pan. If desired, add any or all optional ingredients. Cover with water and wine. Bring to boil, reduce heat and simmer uncovered for 20 minutes. Turn off heat and allow to cool. Strain stock.

90 Mussels in Cream

Lobster Sauté with Guacamole Sauce

TOWN FARMS INN
Middletown, Connecticut

4 SERVINGS

SAUCE

  4 cups half and half
  ½ cup (1 stick) butter
  ½ cup flour
  2 tablespoons Worcestershire sauce
  1 tablespoon minced onion
  1 garlic clove, minced, or ⅛ teaspoon garlic powder
  ¼ teaspoon salt
    Dash white pepper

MUSSELS

 40 mussels, scrubbed and rinsed, beards removed
  1 cup (2 sticks) butter, cut into small pieces
  1 cup dry white wine
  2 tablespoons minced fresh parsley

FOR SAUCE: In 2-quart saucepan, heat half and half; do not boil. In small saucepan, melt butter and stir in flour with whisk to make roux. Cook over low heat, stirring constantly, for 2 to 3 minutes. Do not permit roux to change color. Whisk into heated cream. Season with Worcestershire sauce, onion, garlic, salt and pepper. Simmer 30 minutes, whisking occasionally. Strain and set aside.

FOR MUSSELS: Place mussels in 8-quart or larger heavy saucepan or kettle. Add butter and wine and heat until butter is melted. Cover and simmer until mussels open, about 3 to 5 minutes. Discard any mussels which do not open. Add cream sauce and parsley and serve mussels immediately in large tureen or individual bowls with sauce poured over.

TANQUE VERDE RANCH
Tucson, Arizona

6 TO 8 SERVINGS

  ¼ cup (½ stick) butter
  3 pounds uncooked lobster meat, thickly sliced or in 1-inch-thick chunks
    Salt and white pepper
  1 large garlic clove, finely minced
    Guacamole Sauce*
    Avocado slices; black olives, sliced; tomatoes, diced and peeled or pomegranate seeds (optional garnish)

In 12-inch skillet, melt butter over low heat. Add lobster meat, salt and pepper to taste and garlic. Cook over medium heat until meat just turns pink, about 20 minutes. Place lobster in warm chafing dish or directly onto warm serving plates. Spoon Guacamole Sauce over lobster. If desired, garnish top with avocado slices, sliced olives, diced peeled tomatoes, or sprinkle with pomegranate seeds.

*Guacamole Sauce

6 TO 8 SERVINGS

  4 large ripe avocados
4–6 tablespoons fresh lime juice
    Salt
  1 teaspoon ground coriander, or 2–3 tablespoons chopped fresh cilantro (coriander)
  2 large tomatoes, peeled, seeded and chopped
  ¼ cup minced onion
  2 garlic cloves, finely minced or pressed
  3 drops hot pepper sauce

Peel, halve, and pit avocados. In bowl, mash flesh coarsely with fork, blending in lime juice. Add salt to taste, coriander, tomatoes, onion, garlic and pepper sauce. Mix gently and spoon over sautéed lobster.

Filleting salmon looks easy when the chef at the John Hancock Inn, in Hancock, New Hampshire, does it. Just start at the tail with a sharp knife and cut along the spine to the head.

Curried Shrimp with Orange Rice

Shrimp Scampi

CHALET SUZANNE
Lake Wales, Florida

4 TO 6 SERVINGS

SHRIMP
- ⅓ cup (scant ¾ stick) butter or margarine
- 3 tablespoons flour
- 1½ teaspoons curry powder or to taste
- ½ teaspoon salt
- ¼ teaspoon paprika
  Dash nutmeg
- 2 cups half and half
- 1 tablespoon finely chopped candied ginger
- 1 tablespoon freshly squeezed lemon juice
- 1 teaspoon dry sherry
- 1 teaspoon onion juice
  Dash Worcestershire sauce
- 3 cups (about 25) medium raw shrimp, cleaned and cut in half lengthwise

ORANGE RICE
- 2 cups long grain rice
- 1 cup orange juice
- 2 tablespoons freshly grated orange peel

GRILLED PINEAPPLE RINGS
- 6–8 slices canned pineapple, well drained
- 2–3 tablespoons sugar
- 2 tablespoons (¼ stick) butter

FOR SHRIMP: In 1½- to 2-quart saucepan, melt butter or margarine. Blend in flour, curry powder, salt,

paprika and nutmeg. Gradually stir in half and half. Cook over medium heat until sauce thickens, stirring constantly with wire whisk. Stir in ginger, lemon juice, sherry, onion juice and Worcestershire sauce. Bring mixture to low simmer and add shrimp all at once. Cover, turn off heat and wait until shrimp are pink and completely opaque but soft, about 3 minutes. Stir and serve on or with orange rice, topped with grilled pineapple rings.

FOR ORANGE RICE: Cook rice according to package directions. Do not overcook. When rice is done add juice and peel; mix lightly. Serve hot.

FOR GRILLED PINEAPPLE RINGS: Dip both sides of pineapple in sugar. In large skillet or sauté pan, melt butter and sauté pineapple until golden brown on underside. Turn and brown second side.

If desired, curry may be served with condiments such as chutney, chopped salted peanuts, chopped parsley, crisp bacon bits, flaked coconut, finely chopped orange peel, slivered crystallized ginger, finely minced onion, orange marmalade and chopped mango.

THE VICTORIAN
Whitinsville, Massachusetts

FOR EACH SERVING
- 6 uncooked medium shrimp
- 2 tablespoons olive oil
- 1 garlic clove, crushed
- ¼ cup dry white vermouth
- 1–2 tablespoons fresh breadcrumbs
- 1 teaspoon minced fresh parsley
- ½ small lemon, cut in wedges

Peel and devein shrimp, leaving tail section intact. Wash shrimp under running water; pat dry with paper towel. In 8-inch skillet, heat olive oil over high heat; do not allow to smoke. Add shrimp, cook until shrimp become opaque, about 2 minutes. Add garlic and cook until shrimp are pink. Add vermouth, and ignite with a match until vermouth flames. Shake skillet to loosen shrimp and tip to let wine accumulate on one side. Add breadcrumbs gradually, enough to thicken liquid, but not to make sauce pasty. Remove shrimp to serving platter, pour sauce over, sprinkle with parsley and garnish with lemon wedges.

A VICTORIAN INN WITH FRENCH CUISINE

The Victorian has style—both in its carefree elegance, which is straight out of the 19th century, and in its superb French cuisine, meticulously prepared and served. The inn is a Victorian mansion, midway between Worcester, Massachusetts, and Providence, Rhode Island, that was once the property of a local cotton mill owner. It was restored to its present state of museum-like perfection by a young couple, Orin and Martha Flint. Martha is *chef extraordinaire*.

Baked Stuffed Shrimp

THE PUBLICK HOUSE
Sturbridge, Massachusetts

6 SERVINGS

18 jumbo raw shrimp, shelled and deveined
⅓ cup finely minced scallops
4 cups fresh breadcrumbs
¼ cup freshly grated Romano cheese
3 tablespoons finely crushed potato chips
1 teaspoon paprika
¼ cup (½ stick) butter, melted
¼ cup dry sherry
1 tablespoon water
Lemon Butter*

Split shrimp lengthwise deeply enough to almost pierce backs. Wash thoroughly. Spoon about 1 teaspoon scallops between halves of each shrimp. Arrange shrimp in shallow 13 × 9-inch greased baking dish; set aside.

Preheat oven to 350°F. In large bowl, mix together breadcrumbs, Romano cheese, potato chips and paprika. Add butter and sherry and mix well. Pat some of mixture over each shrimp. Sprinkle 1 or 2 drops water over each shrimp to prevent drying. Bake uncovered for 20 minutes. Spoon Lemon Butter over each shrimp before serving.

*Lemon Butter

6 SERVINGS

½ cup (1 stick) butter
⅓ cup beef stock or canned beef bouillon
1½ tablespoons Worcestershire sauce
Juice of 2 lemons
¼ teaspoon salt

In small saucepan, brown butter over low heat. Cool to room temperature. Add stock or bouillon, Worcestershire sauce, lemon juice and salt. Mix thoroughly, but do not reheat.

Tofu with Sautéed Vegetables

WHEATLEIGH
Lenox, Massachusetts

4 TO 6 SERVINGS

1–2 tablespoons cooking oil
2 teaspoons tamari*
Juice of 2 lemons
4 garlic cloves
2 teaspoons finely chopped ginger root
2 teaspoons curry powder or to taste
1 teaspoon finely chopped fresh basil or ½ teaspoon dried
Pinch ground red pepper
5 cakes Chinese tofu (bean curd), drained and sliced in ¼-inch-thick slices
1 head broccoli, stems sliced diagonally in ¼-inch-thick slices and head broken into florets
1 pound mushrooms, sliced
¼ cup water

In 12-inch heavy skillet, cover bottom with oil and tamari. Heat skillet slowly, adding lemon juice. When skillet is hot, add garlic, ginger, curry powder, basil and red pepper. Cook 1 to 2 minutes to develop flavors. Remove garlic cloves if desired. Add tofu, in 2 layers if necessary. Over medium heat, cook tofu until bottom layer is golden brown. Use spatula to turn tofu and cook other side until golden brown. Add broccoli, stems first, then florets, mushrooms and water. Turn heat low and simmer, covered, until broccoli stems are crisp-tender, about 3 to 5 minutes. Broccoli should retain its high green color. Spoon sauce from pan over vegetables and serve hot, with either noodles, spinach pasta, whole wheat pasta or brown rice.

* A low-salt soy sauce available in natural food stores.

SOUPS

"Soup of the evening, beautiful soup!" sang the Mock Turtle in Alice in Wonderland, *and beautiful soup may be a meal in itself or the perfect beginning of a memorable dinner. Innkeepers are busy people, but most of them lavish attention on their kitchens, from which come these splendid soups. Chilled soups in summer, hot and hearty soups when the snow falls. Their secret is time—the time they willingly take to simmer rich stock for hours, to select choice vegetables (or grow them in their own gardens), to use only the best ingredients. Homemade is the key word—a word some city dwellers have lost, alas, from their vocabularies. Yes, country inns may well be the last purveyors of truly "beautiful soup."*

Cheddar Cheese Soup

GATEWAYS INN
Lenox, Massachusetts

6 TO 8 SERVINGS

    4 tablespoons (½ stick) butter
    4 tablespoons flour
    1½ quarts milk, room temperature
    2 cups chicken stock
    2 cups grated cheddar cheese
    ⅓ cup diced onions
    ⅓ cup diced celery
    ⅓ cup diced carrots
    ¼ teaspoon minced garlic
       Salt and freshly ground pepper
    2 tablespoons sherry

In 4-quart saucepan, melt 3 tablespoons butter. Add flour and stir to make roux. Remove from heat, add milk and stir with wire whisk until creamy. Return to medium heat and add chicken stock and cheese. Let simmer for 15 minutes, stirring occasionally. Meanwhile in 10-inch skillet, sauté onions, celery, carrots and garlic in remaining butter until onions and celery are soft but not brown, about 5 to 10 minutes. Strain soup and return to saucepan. Add vegetables and mix well. Season with salt and pepper to taste. Just before serving, stir in sherry.

Cream of Cheddar Cheese and Vegetable Soup

SIGN OF THE SORREL HORSE
Quakertown, Pennsylvania

10 SERVINGS

    1 cup (2 sticks) unsalted butter
    1 large onion, finely chopped
    1 cup finely chopped celery
    1 cup finely chopped carrots
    1 medium zucchini, finely chopped
    ⅔ cup flour
    6 cups chicken stock
    1 cup whipping cream
    ½ pound sharp cheddar cheese, grated
       Salt and finely ground white pepper
       Croutons (garnish)
       Chopped fresh parsley (garnish)

Melt butter in 4-quart saucepan over low heat. Add vegetables and sauté until tender but not brown, about 15 minutes. Add flour and cook roux, stirring constantly. Add chicken stock, whisking into roux until smooth. Cool slightly. Transfer to blender and puree until creamy, about 30 seconds. Return to saucepan and gradually add cream and cheese. Stir over medium heat until cheese has melted. Season with salt and pepper to taste. Serve garnished with croutons and parsley.

Autumn Bisque

RED LION INN
Stockbridge, Massachusetts

4 TO 6 SERVINGS

    1 1-pound butternut squash, halved, seeds removed
    2 green apples, peeled, cored, coarsely chopped
    1 medium onion, chopped
       Pinch dried rosemary
       Pinch dried marjoram
    4 cups chicken stock
    2 slices white bread, trimmed and cubed
       Salt and freshly ground pepper to taste
    2 egg yolks
    ¼ cup whipped cream

In heavy 3-quart saucepan, combine squash, apples, onion, herbs, chicken stock, bread cubes, salt and pepper. Bring to boil and simmer uncovered until squash is tender, about 30 to 45 minutes. Remove squash, scoop out pulp, discard skins, and return pulp to soup. Puree soup in batches in blender until smooth; return to saucepan. In small bowl, beat egg yolks and cream together. Whisk in a little hot soup, then stir mixture back into saucepan. Reheat, but do not allow to boil.

"At the Pump House Inn," says Mark Kaplan, talented young chef of this Pocono inn that's famous for its good food, "we always add pigs' knuckles and calves' feet, even to our white stock. They add flavor and provide more gelatin than marrow bones alone. When the stock is reduced, it is full bodied and not watery. It should cling to the plate."

White stock is made the same way, using a cut-up stewing chicken in place of beef. "We add bones from a veal breast for added richness," says Mark.

Seafood stock can be made with fish heads, bones and trimmings, or just shrimp and lobster shells, which makes for a lighter broth.

All stock may be frozen for future use in soups, as well as stews, sauces and other savory dishes. Nothing in can or cube can take its place.

Cream of Broccoli Soup

PUMP HOUSE INN
Canadensis, Pennsylvania

8 SERVINGS

- 6 tablespoons (¾ stick) butter
- 2 medium onions, diced
- 2 celery stalks, diced
- 2 garlic cloves, crushed
- 3 pounds broccoli, cleaned and trimmed
- 1 quart chicken stock or bouillon
  Pinch dried marjoram
  Pinch dried thyme
  Pinch dried savory
- 1 bay leaf
- 3 cups whipping cream
- 10 tablespoons quick-cooking tapioca
  Salt and freshly ground pepper
  Garlic-flavored croutons (garnish)

Melt butter in 4-quart saucepan over low heat. Add onions and celery and cook until translucent, about 5 minutes. Add garlic and continue cooking 3 more minutes. Remove broccoli florets from stems and set aside; add stems to saucepan. Blend in chicken stock and herbs. Cover and simmer 1 hour. Transfer to blender in batches and puree. Return to saucepan and add cream and tapioca. Cover partially and simmer 30 minutes. Add broccoli florets and cook until florets are just barely tender, about 4 to 6 minutes. Season with salt and pepper to taste. Serve with croutons.

Carrot and Cashew Soup

WILLIAMSVILLE INN
West Stockbridge, Massachusetts

6 SERVINGS

VEGETABLE STOCK
- 4 cups water
- 1 6-ounce can vegetable juice
- 2 cups chopped celery (stalks and leaves)
- 2 medium leeks, chopped
- 2 large onions, chopped
- ¼ pound green beans, chopped
- 1 large carrot, sliced
- 6 whole black peppercorns
- 1 bay leaf
- ½ teaspoon salt

VEGETABLES
- 1 cup carrots, cut julienne into 2-inch strips
- ½ cup cooked rice
- ½ cup coarsely chopped cashews
  Salt and freshly ground pepper

FOR STOCK: In 4-quart saucepan, combine all ingredients and simmer, covered, for 1 hour. Strain, pressing to extract as much liquid as possible. (There should be 6 cups of stock.)

FOR VEGETABLES: Add all ingredients to stock and cook until carrots are tender, about 20 to 25 minutes. Taste, adjust seasoning and serve.

Green Pea Soup

SALISHAN LODGE
Gleneden Beach, Oregon

10 SERVINGS

- 1 medium onion, chopped
- ¾ cup plus 2 tablespoons (1¾ sticks) butter
- 2 10-ounce packages frozen peas
- 6 cups rich chicken stock
- 2 teaspoons finely minced garlic
- 1 small bay leaf
- ½ teaspoon dried tarragon
- ½ teaspoon dill
- ¾ cup flour
  Salt and pepper
- 1 cup whipping cream, warmed

In 4-quart saucepan, sauté onion in 2 tablespoons butter until soft, about 5 minutes. Add peas, chicken stock, garlic, bay leaf, tarragon and dill and simmer for 25 to 30 minutes. Puree in batches in blender. Strain through fine mesh sieve, return to saucepan and keep warm over low heat. In 1-quart saucepan, melt remaining butter. Stir in flour to make roux. Remove from heat and stir in about 1 cup soup, blending until smooth. Add roux to soup and cook, stirring constantly, until thickened. Season with salt and pepper to taste. Stir in cream just before serving.

Seven generations have lived at the Homestead, a New Hampshire farmhouse converted to an inn in 1880. Esther Tefft Serafini now presides over a true country inn renowned for its home cooking.

Scots Garlic Soup

PILGRIM'S INN
Deer Isle, Maine

6 SERVINGS

 1 medium onion, thinly sliced
 5 garlic cloves or to taste, thinly sliced
 2 tablespoons olive oil
 1 medium potato, diced
 1 green pepper, sliced into thin strips
 4 cups beef stock
 1 8-ounce can tomatoes, coarsely chopped
 ½ teaspoon dried basil or to taste
 ½ teaspoon dried parsley
   Pinch saffron
   Chopped fresh parsley, freshly grated Parmesan cheese and fresh croutons (garnish)

In 3-quart saucepan, sauté onion and garlic in olive oil over low heat. When onion is golden, stir in potato and green pepper and cook for 2 minutes over moderate heat. Add beef stock, tomatoes, herbs and saffron and stir well. Cook until potatoes are done but firm, about 10 minutes. Serve garnished with parsley, Parmesan cheese and croutons.

Swiss Potato Soup with Gruyère

STONEHENGE
Ridgefield, Connecticut

6 TO 8 SERVINGS

 5 or 6 slices lean bacon, coarsely chopped
 1 medium onion, coarsely chopped
 ¼ head white cabbage, coarsely chopped
 1 leek (green stem discarded), coarsely chopped
 1 pound (2–3 medium) raw potatoes, coarsely chopped
 3 cups chicken stock
   Salt and freshly ground pepper
 1 cup shredded Gruyère cheese
 ½ cup half and half
 1 tablespoon finely chopped fresh dill (garnish)

In 3-quart saucepan, sauté bacon over medium heat until just beginning to crisp, about 4 minutes. Add onion, cabbage and leek and sauté for another 5 minutes, stirring occasionally. Add potatoes, chicken stock, salt and pepper and bring to boil. Reduce heat, cover and simmer for 40 minutes.

Transfer soup to blender in batches and puree. Strain soup back into saucepan and keep warm over low heat. Add cheese small amount at a time and stir until melted. Do not boil. Just before serving, adjust seasoning, stir in half and half and sprinkle with dill.

Zucchini Soup

SALISHAN LODGE
Gleneden Beach, Oregon

12 SERVINGS

 ¼ cup (½ stick) butter
4–5 large zucchini, peeled and coarsely chopped
 1 large onion, coarsely chopped
 2 carrots, coarsely chopped
 2 garlic cloves
 1 bay leaf
 1 teaspoon marjoram
 2 quarts chicken stock
 1 bunch sweet-tasting watercress, stemmed*
2–3 zucchini, diced (optional garnish)
 ½ cup (1 stick) butter
 ½ cup flour
 1 pint light cream
   Salt and pepper

In 6- to 8-quart saucepan over low to medium heat, melt ¼ cup butter and sauté zucchini, onion and carrots until onion is translucent, about 5 to 7 minutes. Do not brown. Add garlic, bay leaf and marjoram. Add chicken stock and simmer until vegetables are quite tender, about 20 to 30 minutes. Stir in watercress. Transfer to blender and puree thoroughly. If smoother texture is desired, pass puree through strainer. If using diced zucchini as garnish, add now. In 3-cup saucepan, melt remaining butter and stir in flour to make roux. Add to soup mixture. Simmer for 5 minutes, stirring constantly as roux cooks and thickens soup. Stir in cream. Season with salt and pepper to taste.

* If watercress is bitter, omit.

Home cooks often overlook wine as a natural enhancer of soup, or think that a splash of cooking wine will magically change the soup's flavor. In fact, an inferior wine can ruin the cook's best intentions—and soups! Nothing less than the same high quality wine that is served at the table should be used.

Jean Morel, innkeeper-chef of the renowned restaurant-inn, L'Hostellerie Bressane, gives soup his own special touch. "Everyone serves onion soup," he says, "but no one adds egg yolks, Madeira and cognac." The Copper Beech Inn adds sherry to its Lobster Bisque, a wine that also improves black bean and lentil soups.

Wine adds needed zest to cold soups, too. The Flying Cloud Inn uses white wine in its Cold Strawberry Soup; the Gateways Inn, white wine and sherry in its Cold Cranberry Soup. And the Williamsville Inn's unusual Cold Cantaloupe Soup gains flavor from white vermouth and brandy.

Famous Vegetable Chowder

THE HOMESTEAD
Sugar Hill, New Hampshire

8 TO 10 SERVINGS

CONSOMMÉ
- 3 pounds beef bones or combined beef and veal bones
- 2 large onions, sliced
- 2 cups leafy ends celery, leaves attached
- 1 teaspoon salt
  Water to cover
  Salt to taste

VEGETABLES
- ½ cup (1 stick) margarine or olive oil
- 1 cup chopped carrots
- 1 cup chopped onions
- 1 cup chopped celery
- 1 cup chopped bell peppers
- 1 10-ounce package frozen lima beans or 1½ cups fresh lima beans, shelled
- 3 small white turnips, diced
- 1 16-ounce can stewed tomatoes
- 1 8-ounce package macaroni or other pasta
  Freshly grated Parmesan cheese (garnish)

FOR CONSOMMÉ: In 6-quart or larger soup kettle, combine bones with onions, celery and 1 teaspoon salt. Cover well with water and simmer uncovered until consommé is strongly flavored, about 3 hours. Remove bones and strain into clean kettle. Bring to simmer and salt to taste.

FOR VEGETABLES: In 10-inch skillet containing margarine or olive oil, sauté carrots, onions, celery and peppers until onions begin to lightly brown, about 10 to 15 minutes. Add to consommé. Add lima beans, turnips and stewed tomatoes. Simmer until lima beans are tender, about 20 to 25 minutes. Meanwhile cook macaroni according to package directions. Drain and add to chowder. Serve hot in large soup bowls with sprinkling of grated cheese.

Soup will develop fuller flavor if tablespoon of grated Parmesan is stirred in and soup is permitted to stand 1 or 2 hours before serving. Reheat before serving.

Tomato Soup with Wine

STAFFORD'S-IN-THE-FIELDS
Chocorua, New Hampshire

6 TO 8 SERVINGS

For this soup, seasoning with salt and pepper may be left to individuals at table.

- 2 large tomatoes, peeled and finely chopped
- ½ cup minced onion
- 3 tablespoons (⅜ stick) butter
- 2 cups rich chicken stock
- 1 cup dry white wine
- ¼ cup chopped fresh mint

In 1½-quart saucepan, cook tomatoes and onion slowly in butter until soft. Add stock and wine and simmer 15 minutes. Just before serving, add mint. Serve hot.

Lenora Bowen, chef at the Williamsville Inn, West Stockbridge, Massachusetts, "can't bear to throw anything away" and says that soups are a great way to use leftovers. Even slightly wilted lettuce has a place in soups. Her suggestions for varying the Minted Romaine Soup recipe are:

Broccoli soup with dry mustard and mace
Green bean soup with summer savory and mace
Zucchini soup with fresh dill, garlic and lemon juice
Spinach soup with lemon juice, mace, and chervil

Peanut Soup

RED FOX TAVERN
Middleburg, Virginia

12 TO 14 SERVINGS

- 1 medium onion, minced
- 2 celery stalks, finely chopped
- ⅓ cup (⅔ stick) butter
- ⅓ cup flour
- 3 quarts chicken stock
- 3 cups creamy peanut butter
- 2 cups milk, warmed
- 2 cups half and half, warmed
  Dash Worcestershire sauce
- ½ cup chopped roasted peanuts (garnish)

In heavy 6-quart saucepan, sauté onion and celery in butter until tender. Add flour and stir until smooth. Slowly add stock, stirring constantly, and bring to boil. Add peanut butter, mixing well. Reduce heat, add milk and half and half and stir constantly until well blended and heated through, about 3 minutes. Stir in Worcestershire sauce. Transfer to tureen or individual bowls and garnish with peanuts.

Minted Romaine Soup

WILLIAMSVILLE INN
West Stockbridge, Massachusetts

6 TO 8 SERVINGS

- 3 tablespoons (⅜ stick) unsalted sweet butter
- 1 medium onion, chopped
- 2 tablespoons flour
- 4 cups chicken stock, broth or bouillon
- 4 cups coarsely chopped romaine* (approximately 1 medium head, including outside leaves)
- 1 teaspoon chopped fresh mint
- 1 cup whipping cream
  Salt and white pepper
- ½ cup sour cream (for cold soup)

In 3-quart saucepan, melt butter and cook onion gently until translucent, about 5 minutes; do not brown. Sprinkle in flour and blend with whisk until smooth. Cook gently for 2 minutes. Add stock slowly, whisking to blend. Bring to low boil and add romaine and mint. Cook until romaine wilts, about 5 minutes. Transfer in batches to blender or processor and mix until smooth. Return to saucepan and stir in cream. Season with salt and pepper to taste.

Serve hot or cold. For cold soup, refrigerate at least 4 hours, then whisk in sour cream and serve in chilled bowls.

* Other types of lettuce can also be used.

Carrot and Orange Soup (or Mystery Soup)

PILGRIM'S INN
Deer Isle, Maine

4 TO 6 SERVINGS

Ingredients should be combined carefully so none predominates. The result will be a perfectly balanced synthesis of flavors.

- 2 tablespoons (¼ stick) butter
- ½ cup sliced or chopped onion
- 2 teaspoons freshly ground ginger (or 1 teaspoon dried)
- 1 pound carrots, thinly sliced
- 3 cups chicken broth
- 1 6-ounce can frozen orange juice concentrate, thawed
  Salt and white pepper

In 3-quart saucepan over low heat, melt butter. Add onion and ginger, stirring to coat with butter. Cover and steam gently until onions are wilted, about 3 minutes. Remove cover. Add carrots and chicken broth and cook until carrots are tender. Cool. Puree soup in blender. Return soup to saucepan. Gradually blend in orange juice concentrate a little at a time and taste after each addition until desired balance of flavor is achieved. Lightly season with salt and pepper to taste. Chill thoroughly and serve.

Cucumber Soup with Walnuts

GLEN IRIS INN
Castile, New York

2 TO 3 SERVINGS

1½ cups peeled and diced cucumber
2 tablespoons olive oil
1 tablespoon dried dill seed
1 garlic clove, minced or pressed
1 teaspoon salt
¼ teaspoon white pepper

½ cup yogurt
1 cup sour cream
¼ cup chopped, lightly toasted walnuts

In large bowl, combine cucumber, olive oil, dill seed, garlic, salt and white pepper. Let stand 3 hours.

Puree ½ mixture in blender and add to remainder. Stir in yogurt, sour cream and walnuts. Chill for 8 hours before serving.

Cucumber Soup

SALISHAN LODGE
Gleneden Beach, Oregon

6 SERVINGS

4 cucumbers, peeled (reserve peel)
2½ cups water
2 chicken bouillon cubes
1 large onion, diced
3 tablespoons (⅜ stick) butter
½ teaspoon salt
¼ teaspoon pepper
Pinch dill
1 tablespoon flour
⅛ teaspoon white pepper
Juice of ½ lemon or to taste
1 teaspoon Worcestershire sauce

Milk, light cream or sour cream, if needed
Parsley, chopped (optional garnish)
Fresh dill, minced (optional garnish)

In 4-cup saucepan, bring cucumber peels to boil in 2 cups water. Strain, reserving water. Discard peel. Carefully cut solid outer flesh of 3 cucumbers away from soft inner core containing seeds. Cut solid outer flesh into matchstick-size strips. Cut inner soft core into ½-inch cubes. In a cup, dissolve the 2 bouillon cubes in hot water. In 2-quart saucepan, sauté cucumber cubes and onion in 2 tablespoons butter until onion is translucent. Add ¼ teaspoon salt, pepper, dill and dissolved bouillon cubes and cook 10 seconds more. Add water from cucumber peelings and simmer 5 minutes. In small saucepan, melt remaining butter. Whisk in flour thoroughly and cook 2 minutes to make roux. Strain stock into clean 4-quart saucepan. Rub cucumber and onion through sieve.

Return to stock in saucepan and add roux to thicken. Bring to boil and season with remaining ¼ teaspoon salt, white pepper, lemon juice and Worcestershire sauce. Add cucumber strips. Cool soup. Refrigerate for 1 to 2 hours.

Cut remaining cucumber in half lengthwise and remove seeds. Puree in blender. Add to soup. If it is too thick at this point, add enough milk, light cream or sour cream to achieve desired consistency. Since chilling tends to mask flavor, taste soup and adjust seasoning if needed. Serve well chilled with a sprinkling of parsley and/or dill on each serving.

A soup garnish should be esthetically pleasing and complement the soup in texture and flavor. A sprinkling of chopped chives on vichyssoise is traditional, but try a sprig of watercress for a change, as they do at the Copper Beech Inn, home of Connecticut's famous four-star restaurant.

Robert Noir, *chef de cuisine* at the Copper Beech, often serves consommé with a combination of finely chopped turnip and carrot. But his most exotic garnish is undoubtedly Custard Royale Indienne, a custard made with coconut milk instead of the usual liquid and seasoned with a dash of curry powder. "It is the coconut milk that gives it an indescribable flavor," says Robert. Which proves that the best garnish is the creativity of a talented chef.

Instead of the banal crouton to garnish hot consommé, try crepes, plain or stuffed, and cut in strips. Tiny profiteroles make an attractive garnish for seafood soups and taste even better when stuffed with a fluffy salmon soufflé. A refreshing cold fruit soup is even more appealing when garnished with melon balls or with perfect whole berries.

The color photograph opposite illustrates some of the soup garnishes at the Copper Beech Inn.

Potage Sénégalese

COPPER BEECH INN
Ivoryton, Connecticut

4 SERVINGS

- 1 10½-ounce can condensed beef bouillon, undiluted
- 1 10¾-ounce can condensed green pea soup, undiluted
- 1 10¾-ounce can condensed tomato madrilène, diluted
- 1 tablespoon lemon juice
- 1 tablespoon curry powder or to taste
- 2 cups light cream
  Salt
  Pepper
  Apple, chopped (garnish)
  Parsley, chopped (garnish)

In 2-quart saucepan, combine and heat three canned soups to slow boil. Cool soup. In small bowl, combine lemon juice and curry powder into smooth paste. Thin with a little cream. Stir into soup. Blend remaining cream into soup and season with salt and pepper to taste. Chill thoroughly. Serve with apple and parsley floating on top.

Watercress Vichyssoise

COPPER BEECH INN
Ivoryton, Connecticut

6 TO 8 SERVINGS

- 1 quart chicken stock
- 5 medium potatoes, peeled and sliced
- 1 bunch watercress
- 1 medium onion, sliced
- 2 tablespoons (¼ stick) butter
- 1 tablespoon salt
- ½ teaspoon white pepper
- 2 cups light cream
  Watercress sprigs (garnish)

Place all ingredients except cream and garnish into 3-quart saucepan. Cook over high heat until mixture reduces by half. Remove from heat, pour into processor and blend until very smooth. Let cool. Add cream and blend. Adjust seasoning. Chill thoroughly. Serve in chilled soup cups, garnished with watercress.

Chicken Cucumber Onion Soup

THE COUNTRY INN
Berkeley Springs, West Virginia

8 SERVINGS

This soup is delicious hot or cold.

- 2 cucumbers, peeled and diced
- 2 small onions, diced
- 2 cups water
- ¼ pound (1 stick) butter
- 2 10¾-ounce cans condensed cream of chicken soup
- 2 cups whole milk or 1 cup milk and 1 cup half and half
- 1 teaspoon curry powder
  Salt and white pepper

In 3-quart saucepan, cook cucumbers, onions, water and butter over medium heat until vegetables are soft and mushy, about 8 to 10 minutes. Add soup, milk, curry powder, salt and pepper. Continue heating, stirring frequently with whisk to prevent sticking. Bring to strong simmer. Taste and adjust seasoning; if soup is too zesty or too thick, add milk or half and half as needed.

RIGHT:
Soups delectably garnished at the Copper Beech Inn, Ivoryton, Connecticut. Clockwise from top left: Consommé with a *brunoise* of turnip and carrot; Potage Sénégalese with chopped apple and parsley (this page); Watercress Vichyssoise with watercress sprigs (this page); Lobster Bisque with lobster claw meat (*page* 110).

OVERLEAF:
An array of ingredients for the Bouillabaisse recipe from Town Farms Inn, Middletown, Connecticut.
See page 109.

100

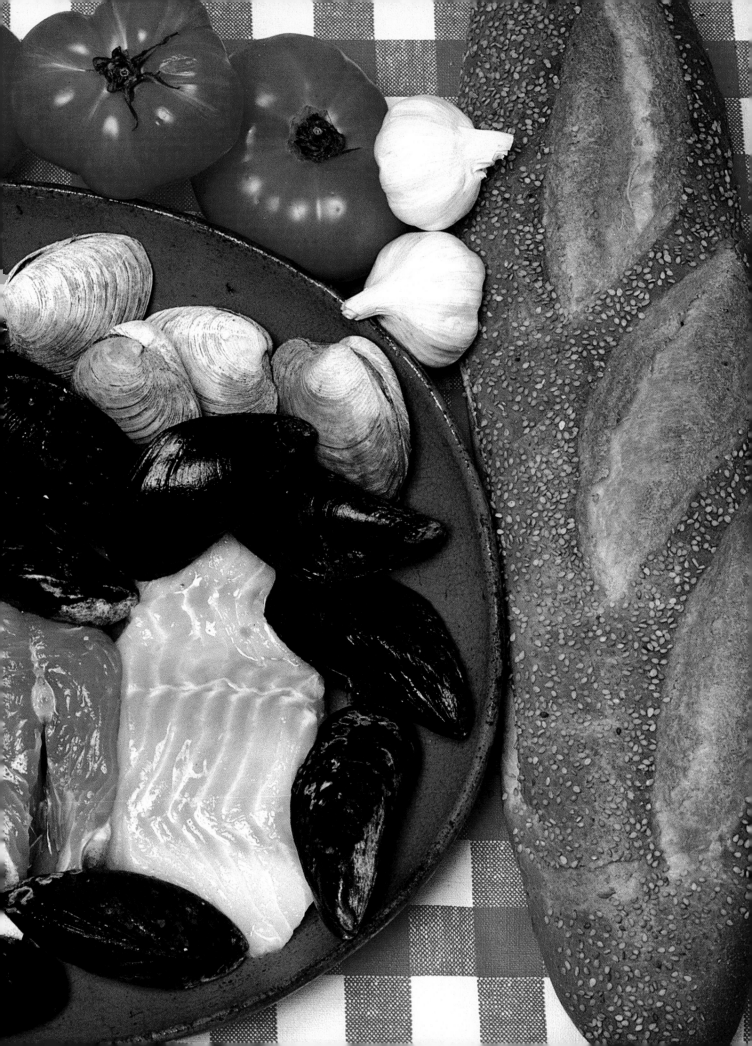

Chalet Suzanne in Florida is noted for its exotic table settings.
This is how a soup of seafood and mushrooms with sherry was served on the day the photograph was taken.
The next day the setting might be different again.

Iced Lemon Soup à la Grecque from Old Drover's Inn, Dover Plains, New York. *See page* 111.

The ingredients for Carrot and Cashew Soup from the Williamsville Inn, West Stockbridge, Massachusetts. *See page 95.*

The ingredients for Autumn Bisque from the Red Lion Inn, Stockbridge, Massachusetts. *See page* 94.

The Bouillabaisse at the Town Farms Inn in Middletown, Connecticut is a rich blend of seafood and vegetables pleasantly spiced. At left is the way the inn serves it and the photograph on pages 102–103 shows the ingredients before the kitchen works its magic.

New England Clam Chowder

PUBLICK HOUSE
Sturbridge, Massachusetts

8 SERVINGS

¼ pound salt pork, ground
1 large onion, finely diced
3 medium potatoes, peeled and cubed
1½ cups water
1 quart chopped clams
3 cups half and half
4 tablespoons (½ stick) butter
Salt and freshly ground pepper

Oyster crackers (garnish)

Cook salt pork in small saucepan over low heat until fat is well melted. Remove cracklings with slotted spoon and reserve. Add onion to saucepan and cook until golden. Remove and set aside. In 2-quart pan, cook potatoes in water until just tender, about 10 minutes. Drain liquid into 4-quart pan. Add clams, cover and cook over moderate heat for 25 minutes. Add half and half, cracklings, potatoes, onion, butter, and salt and pepper to taste and stir until soup is very hot. Serve from bowls with basket of oyster crackers.

OPPOSITE:
Minted Romaine Soup (top) from the Williamsville Inn, West Stockbridge, Massachusetts. *See page 98.*

Cinnamon Strawberry Soup (bottom) from the Flying Cloud Inn, New Marlboro, Massachusetts. *See page 112.*

Bouillabaisse

TOWN FARMS INN
Middletown, Connecticut

4 SERVINGS

½ cup olive oil
5 tomatoes, peeled and quartered
2 leeks, carefully cleaned and coarsely chopped
1 medium onion, thinly sliced
2 garlic cloves, mashed
1 quart Fish Stock*
1 cup dry white wine
¼ ounce saffron
1 teaspoon dry mustard, or to taste
Salt and white pepper to taste
Hot pepper sauce to taste

16 fresh mussels, shells closed and scrubbed clean
12 fresh clams, shells closed and scrubbed clean
8 scallops
½ pound scrod
½ pound halibut
¼ pound salmon
4 large raw shrimp, unshelled
Garlic toast (garnish)

Heat olive oil in 5- to 6-quart soup pot. Add tomatoes, leeks, onion and garlic and simmer until garlic begins to turn golden. Do not brown. Add Fish Stock, wine, saffron and mustard and bring to boil. Turn down heat and partially cover. Gently simmer 5 minutes to blend flavors. Season with salt, white pepper and hot pepper sauce. Set aside 2 cups soup. Ladle remaining soup into warmed large individual bowls or earthenware crocks. Keep warm. Place mussels, clams, scallops, scrod, halibut, salmon and shrimp in soup pan and steam, tightly covered, in reserved 2 cups soup until clams and mussels open, about 5 to 10 minutes. Discard immediately any that do not open. Divide contents of pot among soup bowls. Serve with garlic toast, if desired.

*Fish Stock

MAKES 1 QUART

1 quart water
1 pound white fish bones with trimmings
3 stalks celery, leaves removed
1 onion
1 carrot
½ teaspoon salt
2 dashes white pepper or to taste

In 2-quart saucepan combine fish bones and trimmings, celery, onion, carrot, salt and pepper. Bring to boil and immediately turn flame low. Simmer covered for 25 to 30 minutes, no longer. Cool and strain. Discard vegetables and bones.

Haddock Chowder

MARSHLANDS INN
Sackville, New Brunswick, Canada

6 TO 8 SERVINGS

Tastes best if made the day before to allow full flavor to develop.

- 1 3-inch piece ½-inch-thick fat salt pork
- 1–2 medium onions, diced
- 3 potatoes, diced
  Water
- 2 pounds haddock, preferably with skin and bones (frozen or fresh fillets can be used)
  Salt and freshly ground pepper to taste
- 1 quart whole milk
- 1 13-ounce can evaporated milk

In 6-inch skillet, fry salt pork over low heat until crisp, about 15 minutes. Drain on paper towels. Add onion to skillet and sauté until softened, about 3 to 4 minutes. Put potatoes and onion in top of 4-quart double boiler over boiling water. Add 3 tablespoons fat from skillet and enough water to cover. Simmer covered until potatoes are soft, about 15 minutes.

Season fish with salt and pepper. If using fresh whole fish, cook over low heat in sauté pan with salt pork until fish is tender, about 15 to 20 minutes. Remove skin and bones. Add fish to potatoes in double boiler. If using fillets, add fish to double boiler after potatoes are soft and simmer until fish is tender, about 15 to 20 minutes. Add milk and evaporated milk to fish and potato mixture and heat, occasionally stirring gently, until steaming. Allow to cool, then refrigerate at least 2 to 3 hours or, preferably, overnight. Reheat over boiling water before serving.

Lobster Bisque

COPPER BEECH INN
Ivoryton, Connecticut

6 SERVINGS

- ½ onion, minced
- 4 tablespoons (½ stick) butter
- 1 tablespoon paprika
- 2 tablespoons flour
- ⅔ cup (scant) milk
- ⅔ cup (scant) light cream
- ⅔ cup (scant) water
- ¼ cup sherry
- 2 tablespoons lobster base*
- 2 ounces cooked lobster meat, cut in chunks

In 1½-quart saucepan, sauté onion in 2 tablespoons butter until onion is soft, about 5 minutes. Add remaining butter, paprika and flour. Make roux and let cool. Stir in milk, cream and water and bring to boil. Reduce heat and add sherry, lobster base and lobster meat. Stir gently just until heated through, being careful not to break up lobster chunks. Serve immediately.

* Lobster base is a seasoned concentrated lobster paste available at specialty food shops.

Seafood Mushroom Soup with Sherry

CHALET SUZANNE
Lake Wales, Florida

6 SERVINGS

- 6 tablespoons (¾ stick) butter
- ½ cup plus 1 tablespoon flour
- 2 cups milk
- 3 cups half and half
- 1½ cups uncooked chopped seafood (cod, haddock, shrimp, lobster or combination)
- ½ cup sliced mushrooms, sautéed in 1 tablespoon butter
- 1 hard-cooked egg, finely chopped
- 1 tablespoon salt
- ½ teaspoon grated lemon peel
- ¼ teaspoon white pepper
- ½ teaspoon sugar (optional)
- ¼ cup dry or medium sherry
- 3 hard-cooked egg yolks, sieved (garnish)
- 2 tablespoons chopped chives (garnish)

Melt butter in top of 3-quart double boiler over gently simmering water. Whisk in flour, blending thoroughly. Cook 3 minutes. Add milk and blend. Add half and half, whisking until mixture starts to simmer. Add seafood, mushrooms, egg, salt, lemon peel, pepper and, if desired, sugar. Simmer for 20 to 25 minutes or until flavors are well blended. Add sherry and simmer 5 minutes longer. To serve, pour into hot bowls; garnish with egg yolk and chives.

CHALET SUZANNE

*Wacky, Wonderful and
Out of This World*

Innkeepers Carl and Vita Hinshaw of Florida's Chalet Suzanne, an offbeat collection of pastel turrets and minarets that resembles nearby Disney World. When it comes to imagination, however, Chalet Suzanne's kitchen is the real star.

The inn was founded by Carl Hinshaw's mother Bertha, a Depression-era widow struggling to support herself and two children.

Bertha's soups became so well known that she eventually went into manufacturing, and today her Chalet Suzanne soups are sold in gourmet shops around the world. In fact, the inn's romaine soup was on board Apollo 16 and has been to the moon. The New York Times' restaurant critic Craig Claiborne placed Chalet Suzanne in the first rank of restaurants around the world.

Iced Lemon Soup à la Grecque

OLD DROVER'S INN
Dover Plains, New York

12 SERVINGS

- 4 cups chicken stock
- 2 tablespoons cornstarch
- 2 cups half and half
- 6 egg yolks, lightly beaten
- 1 cup fresh lemon juice
  Dash ground red pepper
- 1 lemon, thinly sliced (garnish)
- 1 tablespoon chopped fresh parsley (garnish)

In 3-quart saucepan, blend small amount of stock into cornstarch and whisk until smooth. Gradually whisk in remaining stock and half and half. Place over low heat and stir constantly until mixture begins to thicken; do not boil. Gradually whisk a little soup into egg yolks, then blend yolk mixture back into soup. Stir in lemon juice and red pepper. Let soup cool; then refrigerate at least 8 hours. Serve very cold, garnished with lemon slices and chopped parsley.

Apple Soup

SQUIRE TARBOX INN
Wiscasset, Maine

6 TO 8 SERVINGS

- 4–5 medium tart apples, peeled, cored and chopped
- 1 small to medium onion, chopped
- 3 cups chicken stock
- 2 teaspoons curry powder
- 1 teaspoon sugar or to taste
- ¼ teaspoon salt
- ⅛ teaspoon white pepper
- 2 cups heavy cream
  Whipped cream, unsweetened or lightly sweetened (optional)
  Nutmeg (optional)
- 6–8 apples, cored and thinly sliced (optional garnish)

In 3-quart saucepan, combine peeled apples, onion, chicken stock, curry powder, sugar, salt and pepper and simmer until apples are soft, about 15 to 20 minutes. Puree in blender. Return to saucepan. Add heavy cream and heat on low flame. Adjust seasonings. If desired, garnish with whipped cream and dust with nutmeg or garnish with thin apple slices. Serve immediately.

May also be served cold. Cool soup and refrigerate for at least 3 hours. Garnish as above and serve.

Cantaloupe Soup

WILLIAMSVILLE INN
West Stockbridge, Massachusetts

3 SERVINGS

- 2 cantaloupes, halved, seeds and skin removed
- 1½ cups fresh orange juice
- ¼ cup dry vermouth
- 1 tablespoon brandy
- ¼ cup sour cream
- ½ cup whipping cream
- ¼ teaspoon cinnamon
  Salt and white pepper
  Sour cream (garnish)
- 3 sprigs fresh mint (garnish)

Puree 3 cantaloupe halves in processor or blender. Pour into large bowl and add orange juice, vermouth and brandy. Whisk in ¼ cup sour cream. Add whipping cream, cinnamon, salt and pepper. Cut remaining cantaloupe half into ½-inch cubes and stir into soup. Divide among glass bowls and garnish each with dollop of sour cream and fresh mint sprig. Cover and refrigerate at least one hour.

GATEWAYS INN

The inn of Gerhard and Lilliane Schmid, in Lenox, Massachusetts, is as justly famous for its superb food as for its luxurious accommodations. Internationally renowned as a medal-winning chef, Gerhard is a master of epicurean specialties. Two of his soup recipes can be found in this section.

112 Cinnamon-Strawberry Soup

FLYING CLOUD INN
New Marlboro, Massachusetts

4 TO 6 SERVINGS

2 pints fresh strawberries, washed and hulled
3 cups water
⅓ cup sugar
2-inch cinnamon stick
Pinch salt
Lemon slice
1 tablespoon cornstarch dissolved in 2 tablespoons water
1 cup whipping cream
½ cup fruity semi-dry white wine (Riesling, Chenin Blanc or Catawba)
Whipped cream or sour cream (garnish)

In 3-quart saucepan, combine berries, water, sugar, cinnamon stick, salt and lemon slice. Boil until berries are soft and have rendered their color. Stir in dissolved cornstarch and cook until thickened. Discard cinnamon stick and lemon slice. Transfer soup to blender or processor and puree. Return to saucepan and stir in whipping cream and wine. Cover and chill thoroughly. Serve garnished with dollop of whipped cream or sour cream.

Cold Cranberry Soup

GATEWAYS INN
Lenox, Massachusetts

8 SERVINGS

2 oranges
1 tablespoon butter
1¼ cups sugar
1 cup sherry
1 pound fresh or frozen cranberries

1 cup dry Sauterne
1 cup half and half
1 cup sour cream
1 cup club soda, thoroughly chilled
16 pecan halves (garnish)

Carefully pare peel from oranges; cut into slivers. Juice oranges; discard membrane and pulp. Melt butter in 3-quart saucepan over low heat. Sauté orange peel gently 2 minutes. Add sugar, sherry and orange juice and let boil 2 minutes. Add cranberries. Cover and boil 2 minutes; uncover and boil 3 more minutes. Let cool, then cover and refrigerate at least 2 hours or, preferably, overnight.

Add Sauterne to chilled soup. Transfer to blender (in 2 batches if necessary) and mix at medium speed 1 minute. Add half and half and sour cream and blend 1 minute longer. Strain into large bowl and chill thoroughly. Before serving, add soda and mix well. Serve in cups over crushed ice, garnishing each serving with 2 pecan halves.

Cold Strawberry Soup

GATEWAYS INN
Lenox, Massachusetts

4 TO 6 SERVINGS

2 pints fresh strawberries, washed and hulled
1½ cups sugar
¾ cup sour cream
1 cup half and half
1½ cups dry white wine (preferably Chablis or Moselle)

Reserve 2 or 3 strawberries for garnish; puree remaining berries with sugar in blender or processor. Strain through fine sieve into 3-quart bowl. Whisk in sour cream, then half and half and wine. Serve in well-chilled cups, garnishing each with halved strawberry.

To increase quantity, add a little more half and half and wine.

VEGETABLES

Lucky the country inn that has its own garden, and fortunately, many do. "We raised ten varieties of lettuce last summer," reports the cook at the Flying Cloud Inn, New Marlboro, Massachusetts. The garden of Block Island's 1661 Inn was the only source of greens for the whole island when a storm cut off ferry service from the mainland.

Inns without gardens are often located near farms, where innkeepers or their chefs may select fresh produce daily. "We buy our salad greens from a local outlet," says Joyce Kaufman of Pennsylvania's Inn at Phillips Mill. "For salads, nothing surpasses Bibb lettuce. Iceberg—never!"

A tossed salad made with a variety of greens is always popular and might include romaine, with long, crisp leaves, watercress or curly chicory and endive, both of which add a tang to milder greens. When young, beet, turnip and dandelion greens are good combined with lettuce, and tender spinach leaves alone make a superb salad, especially with a sharp Roquefort or bleu cheese or a hot bacon dressing.

SHALLOTS, ONIONS, GARLIC AND SCALLIONS

Elaine Wondolowski, chef and innkeeper of the Inn for All Seasons near Boston, celebrated for its four-star restaurant, writes: "Shallots, onions and garlic are related, but each has its distinguishing quality. Shallots are the most subtle and should be used only when briefly cooked—with delicate dishes of chicken, veal and fish, for example. They would be lost in a long-simmered stew, where the stronger onion can hold its own. Onions have a wide variety of uses—as a stuffed vegetable, in the famous onion soup and as an accompaniment and garnish. Garlic, with its notoriously strong flavor and 'remaining' quality, is used in many ethnic cuisines. It predominates in South Italian, is constant in French and is also present

114 Avocado with Celery Seed Dressing

EGREMONT INN
South Egremont, Massachusetts

2 SERVINGS

SALAD
- 1 ripe avocado, peeled, halved and pitted
- 4 leaves romaine lettuce or other salad green, such as watercress, to cover 2 salad plates

DRESSING
- ¾ cup olive oil
- ¼ cup vinegar
- 2 tablespoons plain yogurt
- 1 tablespoon celery seeds
- 1 teaspoon Dijon mustard
  Salt and pepper

FOR SALAD: Slice each half avocado and arrange slices on greens.

FOR DRESSING: Combine all ingredients in jar or shaker. Cover jar tightly, shake well and chill at least 2 hours. Shake again and lightly coat avocado slices. Refrigerate remaining dressing and use for other salads.

Mushroom and Watercress Salad

L'HOSTELLERIE BRESSANE
Hillsdale, New York

8 SERVINGS

- 1–2 bunches watercress, washed and drained
- ½ pound mushrooms, thinly sliced
- 1 teaspoon salt
- ¼ cup white wine vinegar
- ½ teaspoon cracked black pepper
- ¼ cup salad oil
- 1 tablespoon prepared Dijon mustard

Refrigerate watercress. Put sliced mushrooms into a shallow dish. Place salt in small bowl. Pour vinegar over salt and stir to dissolve salt. Add pepper, oil and mustard. Mix well and pour over mushrooms; refrigerate 1 hour.

To serve, pour mushrooms and dressing over watercress and toss.

Spinach Salad

CHALET SUZANNE
Lake Wales, Florida

6 SERVINGS

- 3 cups raw spinach, torn into bite-sized pieces
- ½ cup diced celery
- 5 eggs, hard-cooked and chopped
- ¼ small Bermuda onion, thinly sliced
- 1 clove garlic, crushed
  Salt and freshly ground pepper to taste
- 1 cup sour cream
- 1 package garlic cheese salad dressing mix
- 2 teaspoons freshly squeezed lemon juice

In salad bowl, combine spinach, celery, eggs, onion, garlic, salt and pepper; set aside.

In small mixing bowl, blend sour cream, dressing mix and lemon juice. When ready to serve, blend dressing again, pour over salad and toss well.

in Oriental. All three of these ingredients are in everyday use in fine restaurants, but they are not interchangeable."

Scallions, also called green or spring onions, add piquancy to a tossed salad. They are widely used in Chinese cooking and the tenderest green stems may be substituted for chives.

Wilted Lettuce Salad and Dressing

SQUIRE TARBOX INN
Wiscasset, Maine

4 SERVINGS

- 1 large romaine or head lettuce, separated, washed and crisped (or equivalent amount spinach, watercress, dandelion or other greens, individually or in combination)
- 5 slices bacon
- 2 tablespoons bacon fat
- 1–2 teaspoons sugar to taste
- ¼ cup vinegar
  Hard-cooked eggs, chopped; croutons; green onions, chopped; Bermuda or red onions, sliced (optional garnish)

Place lettuce or other greens in large bowl. In large skillet, fry bacon until crisp. Drain on paper towels and crumble. Remove all but 2 tablespoons of fat from pan, add sugar and vinegar and bring to boil. Pour over lettuce leaves or other greens and sprinkle with crumbled bacon. Toss and serve on unchilled plates, garnished as desired.

Marinated Bean Sprouts and Fresh Mushrooms

INN AT RANCHO SANTA FE
Rancho Santa Fe, California

6 SERVINGS

- Juice of ½ lemon
- 1 teaspoon sugar
- 4 drops Worcestershire sauce
- 1 pound fresh bean sprouts
- 1 pound fresh mushrooms, sliced
- 2 green peppers, finely diced
- 1 onion, finely diced
- 1 2-ounce can pimientos, drained and finely diced

In small bowl, whisk together lemon juice, sugar and Worcestershire sauce. In large bowl, combine and toss vegetables. Pour liquid over vegetables and toss again. If desired, refrigerate 1 hour before serving. Toss at least once before serving to coat evenly with marinade.

Curried Kidney Beans

TAUGHANNOCK FARMS INN
Trumansburg, New York

8 SERVINGS
This can be served either as a relish or a rich salad.

- 1 15-ounce can red kidney beans, thoroughly drained
- ½ cup coarsely chopped celery
- ¼ large red onion, chopped

DRESSING
- ½ cup thick mayonnaise
- ½ cup sour cream
- 1 teaspoon curry powder
  Dash Worcestershire sauce
  Dash hot red pepper sauce
  Lemon juice to taste

In large bowl, mix beans, celery and onion.

In smaller bowl, combine all dressing ingredients until well blended. Add sufficient dressing to lightly coat kidney bean mixture. Cover and chill. Stir well before serving.

For years we were told to cook green vegetables in as little water as possible and serve them the minute they were done. But Joyce Kaufman, innkeeper, together with husband Bruce, of the intimate Inn at Phillips Mill in New Hope, Pennsylvania, prefers today's French method used by her chef. He cooks green vegetables in a large quantity of boiling water until just tender, then plunges them into cold water to stop the cooking and retain the fresh color and texture. They may then be tossed in a little butter and chopped fresh herbs and served immediately or, often more convenient for restaurants and dinner parties, set aside and reheated at serving time.

"Vegetables are very important," says Mrs. Kaufman. "Here, at Phillips Mill, we take as much care in their preparation as we do with the meat they accompany. If the vegetables are overcooked and soggy, no matter how good the rest of the food, the meal is ruined for me."

The Pilgrim's Inn in Deer Isle, Maine, is typical of many country inns in that it maintains a kitchen garden to ensure that vegetables brought to the

---

116 Summer Delight

PILGRIM'S INN
Deer Isle, Maine

8 SERVINGS

May be served as a frozen fruit salad on salad greens or as dessert with a dollop of whipped cream.

- 1 cup sour cream
- 1 8-ounce package cream cheese, room temperature
- ½ cup sugar
- ¼ teaspoon salt
- 1 grapefruit, sectioned
- 1 avocado, diced
- 1 cup seedless white grapes
- ½ cup pecan pieces

In medium bowl using electric mixer, blend sour cream into cream cheese. Blend in sugar and salt. Fold in grapefruit, avocado, grapes and pecans. Pour into 9 × 5-inch loaf pan and freeze just until firm. Slice and serve.

VARIATION: When serving as dessert, substitute blanched, chopped or slivered almonds for pecans and add ½ teaspoon almond extract.

Poppy Seed Dressing

SQUIRE TARBOX INN
Wiscasset, Maine

MAKES ABOUT 3 CUPS

Anne McInvale says this dressing is "super with any kind of fruit. I serve it on mixed fruit salad made with every seasonal fruit I can find. I also use it on salad made of orange slices and onion rings."

- 1½ cups sugar
- 2 teaspoons dry mustard
- 2 teaspoons salt
- ⅔ cup vinegar
- 3 tablespoons onion juice (about ⅔ medium onion, grated)
- 2 cups salad oil (preferably corn or other sweet light oil, but not olive oil)
- 3–4 tablespoons poppy seeds

In medium bowl of electric mixer, combine sugar, mustard, salt and vinegar and mix well. Blend in onion juice. With mixer at medium speed, add oil very slowly, a teaspoon at a time, beating constantly until all oil is added. Add poppy seeds and beat until mixture is well blended and thickened, 2 to 3 minutes. Store dressing in tightly covered jar(s) in refrigerator until ready to use. If dressing separates, shake well. Spoon over salad.

Avocado and Green Onion Salad Dressing

SIGN OF THE SORREL HORSE
Quakertown, Pennsylvania

MAKES 3 CUPS

This dressing is best with Boston or bibb lettuce.

- 3 green onions, coarsely chopped
- 2 ripe avocados, peeled and seeded
- 1 cucumber, peeled and seeded
  Juice of 1 lemon
- 1 garlic clove
- 2 cups half and half
- 1 teaspoon salt
- ¼ teaspoon white pepper

In processor or blender, combine green onions, avocados, cucumber, lemon juice, and garlic and puree until smooth. Add half and half, salt and pepper. Blend 1 to 3 seconds. Store in tightly closed jar(s) in refrigerator.

Sautéed Red Onions and Carrots

HARBOR HOUSE
Elk, California

4 SERVINGS

- 2 tablespoons (¼ stick) butter
- 2 pounds fresh young carrots, diagonally sliced ¼ inch thick
- 3 red onions, thinly sliced
  Pinch dried basil, crushed

Melt butter over low heat in 4-quart saucepan or sauté pan. Add vegetables, cover tightly and cook over low heat for 15 to 25 minutes. Add basil, cover pan and continue cooking until onions and carrots are fork tender.

table are truly "garden fresh." Serving them is also done with care. They may be presented garnishing the entrée, as at the Inn at Castle Hill; served family style as they are at Chesapeake House; or mixed together in intricate assemblies to stimulate the eye and the palate, as in the Aubergine Provençale prepared at L'Hostellerie Bressane (right).

Asparagus Polonaise

GATEWAYS INN
Lenox, Massachusetts

3 OR MORE SERVINGS

- ½ cup (1 stick) butter
- ¼ cup white breadcrumbs
- 1 pound fresh asparagus, freshly cooked
- 2 hard-cooked eggs, chopped medium fine, room temperature
- 1 tablespoon chopped fresh parsley

Melt butter in small saucepan or skillet. Add breadcrumbs and cook until butter foams. Arrange hot asparagus on serving platter. Cover with eggs, then parsley. Sprinkle with breadcrumb and butter mixture and serve at once.

Glazed Carrots

WHEATLEIGH
Lenox, Massachusetts

8 SERVINGS

- 1 cup (2 sticks) butter
- 1 pound dark brown sugar
- 3 pounds carrots, quartered
- 1 bunch parsley, finely chopped

Melt butter in 11- or 12-inch heavy skillet or sauté pan over low heat. Add brown sugar and cook until mixture reaches consistency of heavy syrup. Add carrots, turning until they are covered with glaze. Cook over medium heat until carrots are fork tender. Sprinkle with parsley and serve immediately.

Carrots and Grapes

RED LION INN
Stockbridge, Massachusetts

5 SERVINGS

- 1 small bunch seedless grapes
- 2 cups orange juice
- ½ cup sugar
- ¼ cup semidry white wine (Riesling, Chenin Blanc or Sauvignon Blanc)
- 1 teaspoon cornstarch, dissolved in 2 tablespoons cold water
- Salt and pepper
- 1½ pounds medium-sized carrots, cut in diagonal ¼-inch-thick slices and cooked until fork tender

Wash grapes and drain; set aside. In 4-quart pan, bring orange juice, sugar and wine to boil and reduce heat slightly. Gradually stir in enough dissolved cornstarch to thicken sauce. Cook 1 minute, whisking. Stir in salt and pepper to taste. Stir in carrots and grapes, heat them through and serve.

Aubergine Provençale

L'HOSTELLERIE BRESSANE
Hillsdale, New York

2 TO 4 SERVINGS

- 1 1-pound slender eggplant
- 1 very large tomato
- 2 tablespoons olive oil
- Salt and pepper
- 2 tablespoons breadcrumbs
- 1 garlic clove, minced
- 1 tablespoon chopped fresh parsley
- 1 tablespoon olive oil

Preheat oven to 350°F. With vegetable peeler, peel eggplant end to end. Cut in half lengthwise. Lay eggplant halves on cutting board flat sides down and slice in ⅓-inch slices. Cut tomato in half. Lay flat sides on cutting board and slice thinly. In a shallow baking dish, alternate eggplant and tomato slices. Pour olive oil over vegetables and season with salt and pepper to taste. Bake uncovered until vegetables are almost tender, about 30 minutes. In small bowl, combine breadcrumbs, garlic and parsley. Sprinkle mixture over eggplant and tomato. Drip remaining olive oil over crumbs. Return to oven until breadcrumb topping is browned, about 3 minutes.

118 Eggplant Casserole

THE CHALFONTE
Cape May, New Jersey

4 SERVINGS

    1 cup water, lightly salted
    1 eggplant, peeled and diced
    1 medium onion, chopped
    2 tablespoons (¼ stick) butter
    ¼ cup breadcrumbs

    1 8-ounce can tomatoes, drained
    ½ cup Béchamel Sauce
      (*see page* 175)
    1 tablespoon bacon fat drippings
    1 tablespoon Worcestershire sauce
      Salt and pepper to taste
    ½ cup grated sharp American or
      cheddar cheese
    ¼ cup (approximately) breadcrumbs
    ¼ teaspoon paprika

In 2-quart covered saucepan, place water and boil eggplant and onion until soft without losing shape, about 15 to 25 minutes. Drain in fine sieve. Butter 2- to 3-quart casserole and sprinkle ¼ cup breadcrumbs over bottom and sides; set casserole aside.

Preheat oven to 400°F. In bowl, combine eggplant and onion with tomatoes, Béchamel Sauce, bacon fat, Worcestershire sauce, salt and pepper. Spoon mixture into casserole. In bowl, mix grated cheese, remaining breadcrumbs and paprika. Sprinkle evenly over top of mixture in casserole. Bake until cheese is melted and top is nicely browned, about 10 minutes.

Stuffed Tomatoes

PUMP HOUSE INN
Canadensis, Pennsylvania

4 SERVINGS

    2 firm large tomatoes, unpeeled
    ¼ cup dry breadcrumbs
    1 teaspoon butter, melted
    ½ teaspoon grated Parmesan cheese
    ½ teaspoon finely diced ham
    ⅛ teaspoon leaf basil, crumbled
    ⅛ teaspoon leaf oregano, crumbled
    1 teaspoon minced parsley
      Pinch salt

Preheat oven to 350°F. Cut tomatoes in half. In small bowl, mix remaining ingredients thoroughly and press on top of tomato halves. In shallow baking dish, bake tomatoes until softened, about 15 to 25 minutes (time will depend on firmness of tomatoes). Topping should be lightly browned. If not, tomatoes may be placed under broiler.

Brown Rice Pilaf

ST. ORRES
Gualala, California

4 TO 6 SERVINGS

    2 cups brown rice
    3 cups water or chicken stock
    2 tablespoons (¼ stick) butter
    2 teaspoons salt
    3 bay leaves
    6 peppercorns
    2 tablespoons cooking oil
    1 onion, sliced
    2 celery stalks, thinly sliced
      diagonally
    2 tablespoons currants
    1 tablespoon finely chopped ginger
    ½ teaspoon cumin
    1½ teaspoons ground coriander
      Pepper to taste
    2 tablespoons tamari* or soy sauce

In large pot, place rice, water or chicken stock, butter, salt, bay leaves and peppercorns. Cover and bring to boil over high heat. Reduce heat and simmer until liquid has been absorbed by rice, about 25 to 35 minutes. Pour oil into 10-inch skillet, add onion and sauté for 3 minutes. Add celery, currants, ginger, cumin, coriander and pepper. Stir into cooked rice. Add tamari or soy sauce and mix well. Taste and add more coriander, salt, pepper, ginger or cumin, if desired.

* A low-salt soy sauce available in natural food stores.

At Middletown, Virginia's, Wayside
Inn, the traditional turkey stuffing is
made with peanuts, a local product
that plays an important role in the
inn's cuisine. Extra stuffing is shaped
with an ice cream scoop and used to
garnish the turkey.

Baked
Stuffed Potatoes

FLYING CLOUD INN
New Marlboro, Massachusetts

8 SERVINGS

    8 large baking potatoes
    1 cup grated cheddar cheese, or
       to taste
    1 cup sour cream, or to taste
  ½ cup (1 stick) butter, or to taste,
       room temperature
       Salt and white pepper to taste
  ½ cup grated sardo (Pecorino Ro-
       mano) or Parmesan cheese
       Hungarian paprika

Preheat oven to 425°F. Wash and
scrub potatoes and prick with fork.
Bake until tender and fork penetrates
easily, about 1 hour. Remove potatoes from oven and cut off top hor-
izontal quarter. Spoon out pulp from
both pieces into bowl. Reserve bottom skins. Mash potatoes while still
hot. Mix cheddar cheese, sour
cream, butter, salt and pepper with
mashed potatoes until smooth.

Reduce oven to 300°F. Spoon mixture into potato skins. If desired,
some mixture may be forced through
pastry bag with star tip to finish tops
of stuffed potato skins. Sprinkle generously with sardo or Parmesan, then
with paprika. Bake until tops are
nicely browned, about 45 minutes.

Sliced Potatoes
Baked in Wine

WINDFLOWER INN
Great Barrington, Massachusetts

6 TO 8 SERVINGS

    6 medium potatoes (about 5 cups),
       peeled and thinly sliced (⅛-inch
       slices)
  ½ cup dry white wine
  ½ cup chicken broth
  ¼ cup (½ stick) unsalted butter,
       melted
  ½ bunch green onions, minced
  ½ teaspoon dried dill
       Salt and pepper to taste
    1 egg
  ½ cup whipping cream
       Paprika (garnish)

Preheat oven to 400°F. Butter
11¾ × 7½-inch 2-quart glass baking dish. Fill with potato slices. In
small bowl, combine wine, broth,
butter, green onions, dill, salt and
pepper. Pour over potatoes (liquid
should come up at least halfway to
top of pan). Cover with foil and
bake until tender, about 40 minutes.

In small bowl, beat together egg,
cream and about 2 to 3 tablespoons
of liquid from potatoes. Pour over
top of potatoes, sprinkle lightly with
paprika and bake until top is brown
and crusty, about 20 minutes longer.

Peanut Stuffing

119

WAYSIDE INN
Middletown, Virginia

9 CUPS

Recommended for turkey, chicken or
pork.

  ¾ cup minced onion
  1½ cups chopped celery (stalks and
       leaves)
  ¾ cup (1½ sticks) butter or
       margarine
    8 cups soft bread cubes
    2 teaspoons crushed sage
    1 teaspoon thyme
  ½ teaspoon pepper
    2 cups coarsely chopped unsalted
       roasted peanuts
       Salt to taste

Preheat oven to 350°F. Grease a
9 × 13-inch baking pan; set aside. In
large skillet, sauté onion and celery
in butter or margarine until tender
but not browned. Stir in about one-
third of bread cubes. Transfer skillet
contents to large deep bowl, add
remaining ingredients and toss together. Turn into baking dish and
bake until lightly crusted and
browned, about 30 minutes.

MARSHLANDS INN

A family house that became a country inn, The Marshlands Inn in Sackville, New Brunswick, Canada, has five grandmothers in its kitchen preparing food the slow, old-fashioned way. Stewed foxberries are available at every meal. Also known as cowberries, these mountain or rock cranberries are native to the area around the inn.

120

Stewed Foxberries

MARSHLANDS INN
Sackville, New Brunswick, Canada

4 SERVINGS

This is particularly delicious served instead of cranberry sauce with turkey or other fowl.

- 2 cups foxberries
- 1 cup sugar
- 1 cup water

Rinse foxberries under cold running water. In 2-quart heavy saucepan, combine sugar and water. Add berries and simmer uncovered until tender and all berries have popped, about 10 minutes. If thicker, more jammy consistency is desired, increase cooking time to 25 minutes. Foxberries have a piquant, pleasantly bitter flavor; add more sugar if desired. Serve either hot or cold.

Fritz Grits

PILGRIM'S INN
Deer Isle, Maine

8 TO 10 SERVINGS

- 4 eggs, separated
- 3½ cups water
- 1 teaspoon salt
- 1 cup quick-cooking grits
- ¼ cup (½ stick) butter
- 2 cups grated sharp
  cheddar cheese

Preheat oven to 350°F. Beat egg yolks with fork. Whisk egg whites until stiff but not dry. Set both aside. In 4-quart saucepan, bring salted water to a boil. Slowly add grits to gently boiling water, stirring constantly until mixed. Reduce heat to medium, cook until grits are soft and mixture has thickened, about 2½ to 5 minutes, stirring occasionally. Add butter and cheese. Gradually add egg yolks to hot grits. Fold in egg whites. Pour into greased 1½-quart baking dish and bake until lightly browned and crusty, about 30 to 40 minutes. Let cool slightly before serving.

Fruit Chutney

MARSHLANDS INN
Sackville, New Brunswick, Canada

MAKES 3 TO 4 QUARTS

- 1½ pounds red or blue plums, pitted and cut into eighths
- 1½ cups cider vinegar
- 3 pounds brown sugar
- 1 pound sultana raisins
- 2 large apples, chopped
- ½ pound candied or preserved ginger in syrup
- 2 large red or green tomatoes, chopped
- 2–3 sweet red or green peppers, chopped
- 1 small onion, chopped
- 2 garlic cloves, finely chopped
- 1 tablespoon mixed ground spices (cloves, ginger and cinnamon)
- 2 teaspoons salt
- 1 teaspoon ground red pepper or to taste

In 6-quart covered saucepan or kettle, cook plums with vinegar until very soft, about 5 to 10 minutes. Stir in remaining ingredients and simmer uncovered, stirring frequently until thick, about 45 minutes. Cool, pour into sterilized jars and seal.

BREADS

Fresh bread every day is one of the pleasures of country inn dining, and the variety of recipes that follow indicates the great attention innkeepers pay to homemade breads as part of an inn's attractions.

Marion Brewin, innkeeper at the Rossmount Inn in New Brunswick, makes all the breads herself, while the Publick House in Sturbridge, Massachusetts, employs five bakers who turn out a variety of traditional New England breads, sweet pecan rolls and muffins.

Some inns have specialties for guests to look forward to, such as the Dill Bread that is served at every table at the Victorian in Whitinsville, Massachusetts, and Cissie McCampbell's bite-sized Orange Blossom Muffins, which melt in the mouth of every guest at the Excelsior in Jefferson, Texas.

Chef Anna Rose Newman of the Wayside Inn, Middletown, Virginia, holds a pan of the inn's famous Homemade Bread.

122 Homemade Bread

WAYSIDE INN
Middletown, Virginia

MAKES 2 LOAVES

2 packages active dry yeast
½ cup warm water (105°F to 115°F)
2 cups milk
8 cups flour
½ cup shortening (or 1 stick butter or margarine), room temperature
3 eggs
4 tablespoons sugar
1 tablespoon salt

Lightly grease large bowl and two 9 × 5-inch loaf pans; set aside. In large mixing bowl, dissolve yeast in warm water. Scald milk and cool to lukewarm. Stir milk into yeast. Add 4 cups flour, shortening, eggs, sugar and salt; beat until smooth. Add enough remaining flour to make dough easy to handle. Place dough on lightly floured board and knead until smooth and elastic, about 5 minutes. Form into ball, place in greased bowl, turning dough once to grease all surfaces. Cover with plastic wrap, let rise in warm place until doubled in bulk 1½ to 2 hours. Punch dough down and divide in half. Shape each half into a rectangle, place in bread pans and let rise until doubled, about 1 hour.

Preheat oven to 425°F. Bake loaves until evenly browned and bottom of loaf sounds hollow when lightly tapped, approximately 25 to 30 minutes.

Mrs. Hilda Crockett's Bread

CHESAPEAKE HOUSE
Tangier Island, Virginia

MAKES ABOUT 30 SMALL ROUND LOAVES

8 cups flour
½ cup sugar
⅓ cup lard
1–1½ teaspoons salt
1 package dry yeast
¼ cup warm water (105–115°F)
2–2½ cups water

1 tablespoon butter, melted

In large bowl, mix flour, sugar, lard and salt thoroughly to remove all lumps. Dissolve yeast in warm water, add to batter and mix. Add 2 to 2½ cups water a cup at a time and mix dough with hands until it becomes malleable. Add more water if necessary. Do not knead. Cover bowl with plastic wrap and refrigerate overnight. When ready to bake, form into balls 2 inches in diameter and arrange side by side near outer edge of 6 greased pie pans. Cover loosely with plastic wrap and let rise in a warm place until doubled in bulk, about 2 hours.

Preheat oven to 400°F. Remove plastic wrap from balls and brush tops with melted butter. Bake until lightly browned, about 15 to 20 minutes. Turn out onto racks to cool. May be frozen.

Grammy Tefft's Brown Bread

THE HOMESTEAD
Sugar Hill, New Hampshire

MAKES 2 LOAVES

2 cups yellow cornmeal
2 cups graham flour (whole wheat can be substituted)
½ cup all purpose flour
2 teaspoons baking soda
1 teaspoon salt
1 cup raisins
2 cups buttermilk or sour milk
⅔ cup dark molasses
Butter

Butter insides of two 1-pound coffee cans, tops removed; set aside. In large bowl, combine cornmeal, flours, soda, salt and raisins. In large mixing bowl, beat together buttermilk and molasses. Add dry ingredients and stir until just mixed.

Fill coffee cans ¾ full with batter. Cover open ends of cans tightly with heavy aluminum foil tied with string. Place cans on metal trivet or wire rack on bottom of large kettle. Add about 1 inch water, making sure cans are above water. Bring to boil, reduce heat to simmer and cover tightly. Make sure water will boil slowly enough to produce steam without boiling away too rapidly. Steam bread about 3 hours, checking water level occasionally and adding boiling water as needed. Loaves are done when cake tester inserted through foil into centers comes out clean. Remove foil. Open bottoms of cans with can opener and push out bread. Serve warm with plenty of butter.

CHESAPEAKE HOUSE
Family-Style Meals
on a 17th-Century Island

Descendents of the original British settlers still speak with a cockney accent on Tangier Island, Virginia, home of Mrs. Hilda Crockett's Chesapeake House. Mrs. Crockett is long gone, but her daughters Betty and Edna still serve the same family-style meals, and at night the table is laden with chicken, country ham, freshly grown fruits and vegetables, excellent seafood from local waters and homemade breads. Transportation on the island of 850 people is primarily by bicycle or on foot. Automobiles are as out of place as a store-bought loaf.

Whole Wheat Bread

Dark Bread

PINE BARN INN
Danville, Pennsylvania

PHILBROOK FARM INN
Shelburne, New Hampshire

MAKES 3 LOAVES

- 6 cups whole wheat flour, spooned lightly into measuring cup
- ½ cup sugar
- 4 envelopes active dry yeast
- 2 tablespoons salt
- 4½ cups milk
- ½ cup vegetable oil
- 2 eggs, lightly beaten
- 7 cups all purpose white flour
- 1 tablespoon butter, melted (optional)

Grease 5-quart bowl and three 9 × 5-inch loaf pans; set aside. In large bowl of electric mixer, gently combine whole wheat flour, sugar, yeast and salt. In 2-quart saucepan, heat milk and oil over low heat until warm, 120°F to 130°F. Gradually add to flour mixture together with eggs and beat on low speed until just mixed, about 30 seconds. Continue beating on medium speed for 3 minutes. By hand gradually add white flour, a cup at a time, mixing with large spoon until too stiff to manage. Continue to mix with hands until soft dough is formed. Turn out onto floured board and knead until dough is smooth and elastic. Form into ball. Place in 5-quart bowl and turn to grease entire surface. Cover with damp towel and let rise in warm place, 80°F to 85°F, until doubled in bulk, about 1 to 2 hours. Punch down dough. Divide into 3 equal pieces. Shape into loaves and place in pans. Cover and let rise again until doubled, 30 to 45 minutes.

Preheat oven to 350°F. Bake until loaves are evenly browned and sound hollow when lightly tapped, about 40 to 45 minutes. Remove from pans at once and brush top of loaves with melted butter, if desired. Let cool on rack.

MAKES 1 LOAF

- 2 cups white flour
- 2 teaspoons baking soda
- 1 teaspoon salt
- 2 cups sour milk or buttermilk
- 1½ cups graham flour
- ½ cup dark brown sugar
- ½ cup molasses
- ¼ cup dates (optional)
- ¼ cup raisins (optional)

Preheat oven to 350°F. Grease a 9 × 5-inch loaf pan; set aside. Sift together white flour, baking soda and salt. In large bowl, mix together buttermilk, graham flour, sugar and molasses. Add dry ingredients to this mixture. If desired, add dates or raisins or both. Mix well. Pour into loaf pan and bake until toothpick inserted in center comes out clean and bread sounds hollow when tapped, about 50 to 60 minutes. Remove from pan and cool on rack.

RIGHT:
Dill Bread and the ingredients
for making it were photographed at
The Victorian in Massachusetts.
The recipe appears below.

Whole Wheat Bread (bottom) is one
of several breads made at the Pine Barn Inn,
Danville, Pennsylvania. The recipe
appears on page 123.

124 Healthy Molasses Bread

JAMES HOUSE
Port Townsend, Washington

MAKES 2 LOAVES

       2 packages active dry yeast
    ½ cup warm water (105°F to
          115°F)
       1 cup quick-cooking oatmeal
       1 cup bran
       1 cup seedless raisins
       2 tablespoons shortening
       2 teaspoons salt
    2¾ cups boiling water
    ¾ cup molasses
       1 cup stirred whole wheat flour
    6¾–7 cups sifted unbleached
          white flour

Grease a large bowl and two
9 × 5-inch loaf pans; set aside. Pour
yeast into warm water. In large bowl,
combine oatmeal, bran, raisins,
shortening, salt and boiling water.
Cool to lukewarm. Add yeast and
molasses. Stir in whole wheat flour
and two cups white flour; beat well.
Gradually add enough white flour to
make a soft dough. Turn out on
lightly floured surface and knead
until smooth, about 10 to 20 minutes. Place in greased bowl, turning
dough once, so all surfaces are lightly
coated. Cover loosely with plastic
wrap and let rise in warm place until
double in size, about 1 hour.

Punch dough down; divide in half.
Cover and let rest 10 minutes. Shape
into 2 loaves; place in loaf pans. Let
rise until double, about 45 minutes.
Preheat oven to 350°F. Bake until
tester toothpick inserted in center of
loaf comes out clean, about 55 to
60 minutes. Remove from pan and
cool on wire rack.

Irish Soda Bread

RED LION INN
Stockbridge, Massachusetts

MAKES 1 LOAF

    3⅓ cups flour
    ⅓ cup sugar
    3½ teaspoons baking soda
       1 teaspoon salt
    ¾ cup (1½ sticks) butter
       2 cups buttermilk
       1 cup raisins (optional)

Preheat oven to 350°F. Grease
9 × 5-inch loaf pan; set aside. In
medium bowl, mix together flour,
sugar, baking soda, and salt. Cut in
butter with pastry blender until mixture looks like coarse cornmeal.
Make a well in center of mixture
and pour buttermilk into well. Mix
with fork until thoroughly moistened dough is formed. If desired, stir
in raisins. Pour batter into pan and
bake until nicely browned and tester
toothpick inserted into center of loaf
comes out clean, about 50 to 60
minutes. Remove from pan and cool
on rack.

Dill Bread

THE VICTORIAN
Whitinsville, Massachusetts

MAKES 3 LOAVES

    1½ teaspoons honey
       2 tablespoons warm water
          (105–115°F)
       1 package dry yeast
       2 cups small curd cottage cheese
       1 cup plus 2 tablespoons warm
          water
       6 tablespoons honey
       2 tablespoons dill seed
       3 eggs
       3 tablespoons oil
       3 tablespoons instant onion
       1 tablespoon salt
    ¾ teaspoon baking soda
       9 cups flour

Butter three 9 × 5-inch loaf pans;
set aside. Stir honey into 2 tablespoons water, then stir in yeast. Let
stand until mixture bubbles, about
4 to 6 minutes. In large bowl, mix
remaining ingredients except flour.
Add yeast mixture. Add flour, 2 cups
at a time, mixing until dough forms
a ball and is still tacky. Place in large
greased bowl and turn to lightly coat
all surfaces. Cover with plastic wrap
and let rise in a warm place until
double in size. Punch dough down,
divide into 3 and put in loaf pans.
Let rise again until double in size.

Preheat oven to 350°F. Bake
loaves until nicely browned and
toothpick inserted in center of loaves
comes out clean, about 45 to 60
minutes. Bread should sound hollow
when thumped on side or bottom.
Remove from pans and cool on rack.

ABOVE:
Peanut Stuffing
from the Wayside Inn,
Middletown, Virginia.
See page 119.

LEFT:
Mrs. Hilda Crockett's Bread
before and after baking,
from Chesapeake House,
Tangier Island, Virginia.
See page 122.

RIGHT:
Avocado with Celery Seed Dressing
from the Egremont Inn,
South Egremont, Massachusetts.
See page 114.

Poppy Seed Dressing shown with fruit salad, for which it is recommended.
From Squire Tarbox Inn, Wiscasset, Maine. *See page* 116.

Stewed Foxberries from Marshlands Inn, Sackville, New Brunswick. *See page* 120.

The Old Mill Inn, Bernardsville, New Jersey, combines olives with radishes and celery
to make a striking hors d'oeuvre that would enhance any table.

Another hors d'oeuvre suggestion from the Tanque Verde Ranch, Tucson, Arizona,
is a simple, mouthwatering plate of olives and cooked asparagus.

OVERLEAF:
The hors d'oeuvre tray at
Salishan Lodge, Gleneden Beach,
Oregon, illustrates the
visual delights that can be
achieved with mixed raw vegetables.

The vegetables garnishing a broiled steak
at the Inn at Castle Hill, Newport, Rhode Island,
illustrate the creative use of vegetables as a
dominant part of a meal. The garniture consists of
(starting with the steak and looking clockwise from
bottom left): Mushroom caps, sautéed; summer squash,
sautéed; braised celery; baked tomato; steamed broccoli;
candied carrots; zucchini halved crosswise, hollowed
out, and filled with white asparagus spears surrounded
with a pimiento ring; steamed cauliflower; watercress;
olivette potatoes, blanched and sautéed in butter.

LEFT:
The Inn at Phillips Mill, New Hope,
Pennsylvania, is known for its
superb vegetables. Illustrated here
is the inn's way of serving them
as garnish for a steak. A further
discussion of vegetables appears
on pages 116–117.

OVERLEAF:
A Strawberry Tart
from L'Hostellerie Bressane,
Hillsdale, New York.
See page 153.

Piecrust from the Inn at Starlight Lake, Starlight, Pennsylvania. *See page* 150.

Raspberry Tarts from Shandaken Inn, Shandaken, New York. *See page* 152.

Canada's Cape Breton in Nova Scotia is an enclave of Scots immigrants who have kept Scottish traditions alive for over 200 years. The region was therefore well suited to one of the most famous Scotsmen of all, Alexander Graham Bell, who built a summer home there at Baddeck, where a museum now commemorates his accomplishments.

Among the great traditions of the Scots are their breakfasts, designed to buffer them against the damp, bone-chilling cold of the Highlands. The Inverary Inn at Baddeck is famous for such breakfasts. Guests savor oatmeal porridge, Scottish oat cakes (the recipe for which appears below), and scones made with sour cream and buttermilk, which are shown opposite in the oven of the wood stove used for baking.

Scottish Oat Cakes

INVERARY INN
Baddeck, Nova Scotia, Canada

MAKES 36 TO 40 SMALL CAKES

    3 cups uncooked quick oats
2½ cups all purpose flour
 ½ cup sugar
 ¼ teaspoon salt
 ¼ teaspoon baking soda
    1 cup (½ pound) lard, chilled
 ¼ cup ice water

Preheat oven to 400°F. In large bowl, blend together oats, flour, sugar, salt and baking soda. Cut in lard with pastry blender or 2 knives, or rub in by hand, until mixture resembles coarse meal. Make a well in the center and pour in water all at once. Blend with a fork. Dough will be moist throughout, but will not hold together.

Divide into 2 portions and roll each into a 10 × 12-inch rectangle, ¼ inch thick. Trim edges square and cut each into twenty 2 × 3-inch rectangles. Bake on lightly greased cookie sheets until golden brown, about 20 minutes. Cool on racks.

OPPOSITE:
Latticed Cherry Pie
and an apple pie from
the Kedron Valley Inn,
South Woodstock, Vermont.
See page 152.

Rolled Oats Bread

KILMUIR PLACE
Cape Breton, Nova Scotia, Canada

MAKES 2 LOAVES

    2 cups boiling water
    1 cup rolled oats
    5 cups flour
    1 cake yeast dissolved in ½ cup
       warm water (80°F to 85°F)
 ½ cup molasses
    1 tablespoon butter, room
       temperature
 ½ teaspoon salt
 ¼ teaspoon cream of tartar

Lightly grease large bowl and butter two 9 × 5-inch loaf pans; set aside. In another bowl, add boiling water to oats and let stand 1 hour. Add flour, dissolved yeast, molasses, butter, salt and cream of tartar. Mix thoroughly to form into dough. If necessary add more oats, not flour. Form dough into a ball; consistency should remain soft, almost tacky.

Place in greased bowl, cover with plastic wrap and let rise in a warm place until double in size, about 45 minutes to 1 hour. Divide dough in half. Turn into loaf pans and let rise until double, about 35 to 45 minutes.

Preheat oven to 350°F. Bake until nicely browned and cake tester inserted in center of loaf comes out clean, about 60 to 75 minutes. Loaves should have shrunken from sides of pan and sound hollow when tapped. Remove from pans and cool on wire rack.

Johnny Cakes

141

TOWN FARMS INN
Middletown, Connecticut

16 SERVINGS

    1 egg
 ½ cup sugar
    3 tablespoons (⅜ stick) butter,
       melted
    1 cup milk
    1 cup yellow cornmeal
    1 cup flour
    1 teaspoon salt
    1 teaspoon cream of tartar
 ½ teaspoon baking soda

Preheat oven to 350°F. Grease 8 × 8-inch square baking dish; set aside. In large bowl, beat egg well adding sugar gradually. Add remaining ingredients one at a time, stirring gently to lightly mix. Pour batter into baking dish and bake until toothpick inserted in center comes out clean, about 30 minutes. Cut into 16 squares and serve hot.

THE CHALFONTE
Southern cooking at its finest

Spoon bread is just one of many Southern recipes prepared by Helen Dickerson and her family at Cape May's Chalfonte, a rambling Victorian hotel that is run like a family summer camp. Helen is head of a clan that has been managing the inn's food service for the past forty years. Her kitchen is so renowned that when Washington dignitaries recently dedicated Cape May, New Jersey, as a landmark town, they ate their meals at the Chalfonte.

142 Spoon Bread

Yankee Corn Sticks

Apple Pie Bread

THE CHALFONTE
Cape May, New Jersey

PUBLICK HOUSE
Sturbridge, Massachusetts

JAMES HOUSE
Port Townsend, Washington

6 TO 8 SERVINGS

  1 cup white stoneground cornmeal
1½ teaspoons salt
  2 cups boiling water
  4 tablespoons (½ stick) margarine, melted
  2 tablespoons flour
  3 teaspoons baking powder
  3 eggs, beaten
  1 13-ounce can evaporated milk
    Bacon grease

Preheat oven to 450°F. Pour cornmeal and salt into a mixing bowl. Add water and mix. Pour margarine over mixture and stir until evenly moistened. In another bowl, mix flour and baking powder with eggs and evaporated milk. Pour eggs and milk mixture into cornmeal mixture and stir until well blended. Grease a 1½-quart casserole or Pyrex baking dish at least 2½ inches deep with bacon grease and pour in batter. Bake until top is lightly browned and tester toothpick comes out clean, about 30 minutes.

MAKES 2 DOZEN

2¾ cups all purpose flour
 ¾ cup granulated sugar
  2 tablespoons double acting baking powder
  2 teaspoons salt
  1 cup cornmeal
1½ cups milk
  1 cup (one 8¾-ounce can) cream-style corn
  2 eggs
 ¼ cup vegetable oil

Preheat oven to 425°F. Place empty corn stick pans in oven for a few minutes until quite warm. Remove and grease generously. Set aside in warm place.

In mixing bowl, blend together flour, sugar, baking powder and salt; stir in cornmeal. In another bowl, blend together milk, corn, eggs and oil; add to dry ingredients. Stir until just moistened throughout. Do not overmix. Fill warm corn stick pans ⅔ full with batter. Bake until lightly browned on top and sticks pull away from sides of pan, 18 to 20 minutes.

8 SERVINGS

  3 cups unbleached white flour
  1 cup sugar
  4 teaspoons baking powder
  1 teaspoon salt
 ½ teaspoon ground cardamom
  1 teaspoon cinnamon
 ½ teaspoon ground cloves
1½ cups milk
  1 egg, beaten
  2 tablespoons salad oil
1½ cups diced, unpeeled green apples

Preheat oven to 350°F. Grease 9 × 5 × 3-inch loaf pan; set aside. In medium bowl, sift together dry ingredients. In large bowl, mix together milk, egg and oil. Gradually stir in dry ingredients until well mixed. Fold in apples. Turn into loaf pan and bake until tester toothpick inserted in center comes out clean, about 1 hour 20 minutes. Remove from pan and cool on wire rack.

The making of bread goes back to prehistoric times, when crushed grain and water were mixed and heated. The Egyptians are credited with the discovery—probably accidental—of fermented bread sometime before the twentieth century B.C. They used a leavening of sourdough kept from a previous batch. Bakers of ancient Greece were renowned, and the Roman Republic established public ovens.

Most bread today is made with a leavening of yeast (a source of B vitamins) and enriched flour. But many peoples still eat unleavened breads such as Jewish matzos, Mexican tortillas and Scottish bannocks made from oat or barley meal and baked on a griddle. Norwegian flatbread (or flatbrod) is popular served with pâtés and spreads.

Cranberry Nut Bread

PUBLICK HOUSE
Sturbridge, Massachusetts

MAKES I LOAF

- 2 cups whole fresh or canned cranberries*
- 2 cups all purpose flour
- 1 cup sugar
- 1½ teaspoons baking powder
- 1 teaspoon salt
- ½ teaspoon baking soda
- 1 egg, well beaten
- 2 tablespoons vegetable oil
  Juice of 1 orange
- ½ cup (approximately) milk
- ½ cup chopped walnuts
  Grated peel of 1 orange

Preheat oven to 350°F and lightly grease a 9 × 5-inch loaf pan; set aside. Wash and drain cranberries and chop them coarsely in processor. Sift together flour, sugar, baking powder, salt and baking soda. In large bowl, blend together egg, oil, cranberries and orange juice. Combine flour mixture with wet mixture. Add sufficient milk to give soft, slightly sticky consistency. Mix well, adding nuts and orange peel. Bake in loaf pan until a tester toothpick inserted in center comes out clean, about 1 hour. (Cranberry stain has no bearing on doneness.)

* If fresh or frozen cranberries are not available, one 16-ounce can whole cranberries may be used. Drain contents carefully through a strainer, removing as much liquid as possible while leaving berries intact. Do not chop or cut berries. Combine and bake according to recipe.

Lemon Bread

RED LION INN
Stockbridge, Massachusetts

MAKES I LARGE LOAF OR 2 SMALL LOAVES

- ½ cup (1 stick) butter
- 1 cup sugar
- 2 eggs
  Grated zest of 1 large lemon
- 1½ cups flour
- 1 teaspoon baking powder
- ½ teaspoon salt
- ½ cup chopped pecans or walnuts, toasted
- ½ cup milk
  Lemon Glaze*

Preheat oven to 350°F. Grease two 8 × 4-inch bread pans; set aside. In medium mixing bowl, cream butter and sugar. Beat in eggs thoroughly. In the following order, add lemon zest, flour, baking powder, salt, nuts and milk, continuing to mix until well blended. Divide batter between greased pans and bake until browned and toothpick inserted in center of loaves come out clean, about 45 to 55 minutes. Remove from oven and spoon Lemon Glaze over bread while still hot. Allow to cool in loaf pans.

*Lemon Glaze

MAKES ½ CUP

- Juice of 1 lemon (from lemon used for zest)
- ½ cup sugar

Combine ingredients and mix well until sugar is completely dissolved.

Pumpkin Spice Bread

PINE BARN INN
Danville, Pennsylvania

MAKES 3 LARGE LOAVES

- 7 cups flour
- 5 cups sugar
- 4 teaspoons baking soda
- 4 teaspoons cinnamon
- 2 teaspoons nutmeg
- 2 teaspoons salt
- ½ teaspoon ground cloves
- 4 eggs, well beaten
- 1⅓ cups water
- 4 cups cooked pumpkin puree or two 16-ounce cans pumpkin
- 2 cups (4 sticks) margarine, melted

Preheat oven to 350°F. Grease three 9 × 5-inch loaf pans; set aside. In large mixing bowl, sift together flour, sugar, baking soda, cinnamon, nutmeg, salt and cloves. In large bowl, mix eggs with water until well blended. Add pumpkin, blend thoroughly. Blend in melted margarine. Make a well in center of dry ingredients and add pumpkin mixture. Mix thoroughly until smooth. Spoon into greased loaf pans and bake until toothpick inserted in center of loaf comes out clean, about 35 to 45 minutes. Remove loaves from pans and cool on rack.

The white flour used most commonly for breads, rolls and pastries and as a thickener in sauces is all purpose which can be bleached or unbleached—the less refined, the more nutritious. Cake flour is a flour-starch blend that makes lighter cakes from recipes calling for baking powder.

But for variety and enhanced nutrition in bread making, try whole wheat, cracked wheat, rolled oats or rye flour. Nancy Philbrook, co-innkeeper and pastry chef at the Philbrook Farm Inn in Shelburne, New Hampshire, makes an unusual and delicious Dark Bread using stoneground graham flour, which is ground whole wheat grain with the bran left in. "It gives the bread a nutty, old-fashioned flavor, unlike any dark bread I know," says Miss Philbrook. Graham flour together with yellow cornmeal are used in Granny Tefft's Brown Bread, baked at the Homestead, Sugar Hill, New Hampshire.

BREADS

144 Spicy Honey Loaf

JAMES HOUSE
Port Townsend, Washington

MAKES 3 LOAVES

    2 packages active dry yeast
 ½ cup warm water
 ½ teaspoon sugar
 ¼ teaspoon ginger
    2 eggs
1½ cups warm milk
 ½ cup (1 stick) butter, melted
 ¾ cup honey
1½ tablespoons coriander
1½ teaspoons salt
    1 teaspoon cinnamon
 ½ teaspoon cloves
    7 cups (approximately) unbleached white flour

Lightly grease large bowl and three 9 × 5-inch loaf pans; set aside. In small bowl, combine yeast, warm water, sugar and ginger. Stir until all is dissolved; set aside. In large mixing bowl, whisk eggs until pale yellow and thick. Beat in milk, butter, honey, coriander, salt, cinnamon and cloves until smooth; blend in yeast mixture. Mix 3 cups flour into this mixture until smooth. Add remaining flour, a small amount at a time, until soft dough is formed. Turn out on lightly floured surface and knead until smooth and elastic, about 10 minutes. Place in greased bowl, turning dough once to coat entire surface. Cover loosely and let rise in warm place until double in size, about 2 to 2½ hours. Punch down and turn out on floured surface; knead lightly, cover and let rest 10 minutes. Shape into 3 loaves; place in greased pans, cover and let rise until double, about 1½ hours.

Preheat oven to 300°F. Bake until browned and toothpick inserted in center of loaf comes out clean, about 45 minutes. Remove from pans and cool on wire rack.

Poppy Seed Coffee Cake

THE MAINSTAY
Cape May, New Jersey

16 TO 20 SERVINGS

    1 cup buttermilk
 ¼ cup poppy seeds
 ½ teaspoon almond extract
1½ cups sugar
    1 cup (2 sticks) butter or margarine, room temperature
    4 eggs
2½ cups flour
    1 teaspoon baking powder
    1 teaspoon baking soda
 ½ teaspoon salt
 ½ cup sugar
    1 teaspoon cinnamon

Preheat oven to 350°F. Grease 10-inch bundt pan; set aside. In medium bowl, mix together buttermilk, poppy seeds and almond extract; set aside. In large bowl, cream 1½ cups sugar and butter. Blend in eggs one at a time, beating well after each addition; set aside. In medium bowl, sift together flour, baking powder, baking soda and salt. Add the dry ingredients alternately with buttermilk mixture to egg mixture, beginning and ending with dry ingredients. Pour half of batter into bundt pan. In cup, mix together remaining sugar and cinnamon. Sprinkle evenly over batter in pan. Cover sugar mixture with remaining batter.

Bake until tester inserted in cake comes out clean, about 45 minutes. Cool slightly before removing from pan. Serve warm.

Yeast is the universal natural leavening agent used in all commercial bread making as well as in homemade breads such as the Wayside Inn's white bread, the Victorian's unusual Dill Bread, and the Scottish Rolled Oats Bread at Kilmuir Place, Cape Breton, Nova Scotia.

Chemical leavens include baking powder, used in the Publick House's Pumpkin Muffins and in Spoon Bread from the Chalfonte Hotel in Cape May, New Jersey. Another, baking soda, in combination with sour milk or buttermilk, leavens the Homestead's Grammy Tefft's Brown Bread and the Red Lion Inn's Irish Soda Bread.

Cream of tarter, beaten with egg whites, increases volume and prevents cakes and meringues from falling when removed from the oven. The Pecan Crunch from the Black Bass Hotel in Lumberville, Pennsylvania, uses the leavening, as does the Lime Dacquoise from the 1770 House, East Hampton, New York.

Apple Knobby Cake

THE VILLAGE INN
Lenox, Massachusetts

12 SERVINGS

2 tablespoons shortening
1 cup sugar
1 egg
1 cup flour
1 teaspoon baking soda
½ teaspoon salt
1½ teaspoons cinnamon
½ teaspoon nutmeg
3 cups diced apples

Preheat oven to 350°F. Grease 8-inch square baking pan; set aside. In large mixing bowl, cream shortening and sugar. Beat in egg. In small bowl, sift together flour, baking soda, salt and spices. Beat thoroughly into creamed mixture. Dough will look knobby or crumbly before baking. Turn into baking pan and top with apples. Bake until thin sugary crust forms on sides and bottom and apples are lightly browned and soft, about 40 to 60 minutes. Layer between apples and crust should be dense and soft with slightly granular texture.

Blueberry Muffins

WILLIAMSVILLE INN
West Stockbridge, Massachusetts

MAKES 18 TO 24 MUFFINS

½ cup (1 stick) unsalted butter
2 eggs
1⅛ cups sugar
3 cups flour
3 teaspoons baking powder
½ teaspoon salt
  Pinch baking soda
1 cup milk
1 teaspoon vanilla
2 cups blueberries
  Sugar (as needed)

Preheat oven to 400°F. Grease two 12-hole muffin pans; set aside. In large bowl, cream together butter, eggs and sugar. Reserve 3 tablespoons flour. In medium bowl, combine remaining flour, baking powder, salt and baking soda. Combine milk and vanilla. Alternately add milk and flour mixture to creamed butter and egg mixture. Place berries in large bowl, sprinkle with reserved flour and turn gently with large spoon until berries are lightly coated. Fold berries into batter. Fill each muffin pan ¾ full and sprinkle tops with sugar. Fill any remaining empty wells ½ full with water. Bake until muffins pull away from sides of pan and turn golden brown and crumb on sides or until tester comes out clean, about 15 to 20 minutes.

FOR APPLE MUFFINS: Use basic recipe, substituting apple juice for milk and peeled diced apples for berries. Sprinkle tops of unbaked muffins with cinnamon and sugar.

FOR CRANBERRY MUFFINS: Use basic recipe, substituting cranberries, washed and chopped, for blueberries. If desired, add more sugar to taste.

FOR RAISIN SPICE MUFFINS: Use basic recipe but omit blueberries. Add ¾ cup raisins, 2 teaspoons cinnamon and 1 teaspoon nutmeg.

FOR PINEAPPLE MUFFINS: Use basic recipe but substitute one 16-ounce can crushed pineapple, well drained, for blueberries. To reserved juice, add enough apple juice or milk to equal 1 cup and substitute for milk used in basic recipe.

FOR BANANA MUFFINS: Use basic recipe substituting 3 mashed bananas for blueberries. Sprinkle tops of unbaked muffins with cinnamon and sugar.

PUBLICK HOUSE
Bread Specialists

The Publick House is an old-fashioned Massachusetts inn whose reputation for breadmaking is unsurpassed. The inn has five bakers on staff to satisfy the numerous visitors to historic Old Sturbridge Village nearby.

Christmas is a special time at the inn, which celebrates the traditional twelve days, culminating in a feast complete with roast suckling pig, roast goose, venison, plum pudding and an 800-pound gingerbread house.

146 Apple Streusel Muffins

CHRISTMAS FARM INN
Jackson, New Hampshire

MAKES 12 MUFFINS

    2 cups flour
    ½ cup sugar
    2 teaspoons double-action baking powder
    ½ teaspoon salt
    ½ cup (1 stick) butter, room temperature
    1 large tart apple, pared, cored and diced (about 1 cup)
    ½ teaspoon freshly grated lemon zest
    1 egg, well beaten
    ⅔ cup milk
    ½ teaspoon freshly grated lemon zest
    ¼ cup chopped walnuts
    2 tablespoons sugar

Preheat oven to 425°F. Sift together flour, ½ cup sugar, baking powder and salt. Cut in butter. Reserve ½ cup of this mixture for crumb topping. Stir together apple and ½ teaspoon lemon zest. Add egg and milk; blend this with flour mixture, stirring lightly until evenly moist. Spoon into 12 greased medium-size muffin cups.

Blend reserved crumb mixture with ½ teaspoon lemon zest, walnuts and 2 tablespoons sugar. Sprinkle over batter and bake until toothpick or wire tester comes out clean, about 20 minutes.

Currant Cakes

STAFFORD'S-IN-THE-FIELD
Chocorua, New Hampshire

MAKES 18 MUFFINS

    1¼ cups sugar
    ¼ cup water
    1 tablespoon ground orange peel
    1 cup currants
    1 tablespoon rum extract
    ½ cup (1 stick) butter
    2 eggs
    2 cups flour
    3 teaspoons baking powder
    ½ teaspoon salt
    ¾ cup milk

In 1-quart saucepan, mix together ½ cup sugar, water and orange peel and bring to boil. Add currants and rum extract; stir well and let cool.
Preheat oven to 350°F. In large mixing bowl, cream butter and remaining ¾ cup sugar and beat in eggs. Add boiled mixture and blend well. In bowl, sift together flour, baking powder and salt and mix, alternately with milk, into creamed mixture. Spoon mixture into greased muffin tins, filling each ¾ full. Bake until toothpick inserted in center comes out clean, 20 to 25 minutes.

Pumpkin Muffins

PUBLICK HOUSE
Sturbridge, Massachusetts

MAKES 24 MUFFINS

    2 cups sugar
    1½ cups canned pumpkin
    3 eggs
    ½ cup vegetable oil
    ½ cup water
    3 cups flour
    1½ teaspoons baking powder
    1 teaspoon baking soda
    1 teaspoon salt
    ¾ teaspoon cinnamon
    ½ teaspoon cloves
    ½ teaspoon nutmeg
    1½ cups raisins
    1 cup coarsely chopped toasted walnuts

Preheat oven to 400°F. In mixing bowl, combine sugar, pumpkin, eggs, oil and water. In another bowl, sift together flour, baking powder, baking soda, salt and spices. Add to first mixture and blend well. Fold in raisins and walnuts. Bake in greased muffin pans until toothpick or wire tester inserted in middle of muffin comes out clean, about 20 minutes.

THE DINING ROOM AT EXCELSIOR HOUSE

Presidents Grant and Hayes entertained in the ballroom, the Barrymores took a suite here when their touring company came to town, but a century ago, the Excelsior House in Jefferson, Texas, faced extinction when local officials had a major feud with railroad baron Jay Gould. Despite Gould's predictions of doom, the town of Jefferson hung on without a railroad, and today Jefferson is a curiosity—an old-fashioned village that has been left somewhere in the 19th century. Fortunately, the majestic old hotel with its high ceilings and expensive antiques was restored to its former glory by the Jesse Allen Wise Garden Club.

148 Orange Blossom Muffins

EXCELSIOR HOUSE
Jefferson, Texas

MAKES 12 MUFFINS

- 1 6-ounce can frozen orange juice concentrate, thawed
- ¼ cup sugar
- 2 tablespoons salad oil or melted shortening
- 1 egg, slightly beaten
- 2 cups packaged biscuit mix
- ½ cup orange marmalade
- ½ cup chopped toasted pecans

- ¼ cup sugar
- 1½ tablespoons all purpose flour
- ½ teaspoon cinnamon
- ¼ teaspoon nutmeg
- 1 tablespoon butter or margarine, room temperature

Preheat oven to 400°F. In medium mixing bowl, combine orange juice, ¼ cup sugar, oil or shortening and egg. Add biscuit mix and beat vigorously for 30 seconds. Stir in marmalade and pecans.

Grease muffin pan or line with paper bake cups. Fill each cup ⅔ full with batter. Combine remaining sugar, flour, cinnamon and nutmeg. Cut in butter until crumbly. Sprinkle over batter. Bake until toothpick or wire tester comes out clean, about 20 to 25 minutes.

Sweet Rolls

PUBLICK HOUSE
Sturbridge, Massachusetts

MAKES ABOUT 3 DOZEN

DOUGH

- 2 cups milk, scalded
- ¼ cup (½ stick) butter, melted
- 3 tablespoons sugar
- 1 teaspoon salt
- 1 packet active dry yeast
- ⅓ cup water (105°F to 115°F)
- 2 eggs, beaten
- 6 cups all purpose flour
- 3 tablespoons sugar
- 1 teaspoon cinnamon

GLAZE

- 1½ cups light brown sugar
- ¾ cup (½ stick) butter, room temperature
- 3 tablespoons light corn syrup
- 3 tablespoons honey

FOR DOUGH: Lightly butter large bowl; set aside. In another large bowl, combine milk, butter, sugar and salt and stir until lukewarm. Soften yeast in warm water and add to milk mixture. Beat in eggs and gradually add flour, a cup at a time. Blend thoroughly and form into ball. Turn out on lightly floured board and knead until very smooth but not sticky, using more flour as needed. Place dough in buttered bowl. Turn completely so all surfaces are buttered. Cover with kitchen towel and let rise in warm place until double in bulk, about 2 hours. Punch dough down. Divide into 3 parts. With rolling pin, roll each third into long strips about 18 × 5 inches. In small bowl, blend together sugar and cinnamon. Sprinkle each strip with sugar and cinnamon mixture. Roll long edge of each strip jelly roll fashion. Cut each roll into about 1 dozen 1½-inch slices.

FOR GLAZE: In large bowl, combine sugar, butter, corn syrup and honey and beat mixture until smooth and fluffy.

Grease three 12-hole muffin tins; set aside. Spoon one scant tablespoon of glaze into bottom of each muffin tin well. Cover with slice of sweet roll dough. Cover muffin tins with kitchen towel and let rise until doubled, about 30 minutes. Preheat oven to 400°F. Bake until nicely browned, about 15 to 20 minutes. Glaze may bubble up through sweet rolls. Remove from oven and invert rolls onto wire rack to cool.

DESSERTS

Dessert—Ah, Dessert
Be it as simple as well-aged cheese with apples or pears, or as sinfully rich as a feather-light cake layered with ambrosial filling and topped with clouds of flavored whipped cream, dessert for many diners is a meal's finest hour. Those with a particularly sweet tooth enjoy the custom of the Chalet Suzanne in Lake Wales, Florida, where they serve a rich crepe Suzanne with orange and lemon sauce before the actual dessert.

The creation of desserts brings out a touch of genius in country inn cooks. Taughannock Farms Inn in Trumansburg, New York is known for its extensive desserts. Guests enjoy the Crème de Menthe Parfait recipe that has been in Nancy le Grand's family for three generations. East Hampton, New York's 1770 House makes an unusual apple brown betty topped with marzipan, while the specials at the Old Drover's Inn, Dover Plains, New York, are raspberry sherbet with cassis and an apple cheesecake covered with walnuts and coconut. At the Sign of the Sorrel Horse in eastern Pennsylvania, the chefs make all the ice cream and are perfecting an unusual lemon walnut variety.

PIES—THE UPPER CRUST OF DESSERTS

The aim of the kitchen at the Heritage House in northern California is to produce good, well-prepared American food rather than elevated continental dishes, and that includes the American dessert favorite—the pie. In fact, even at the Wheatleigh in Lenox, Massachusetts, where the cuisine is French and Italian, the dessert that seasoned guests choose is the homemade pecan pie.

150 Piecrust

INN AT STARLIGHT LAKE
Starlight, Pennsylvania

MAKES TWO 9-INCH PIECRUSTS

  2 cups flour
  ¾ teaspoon salt
  ½ teaspoon baking powder
  ½ cup lard, chilled and cut into small pieces
  ½ cup (1 stick) butter or margarine, chilled and cut into small pieces
  6–8 tablespoons ice water

Sift dry ingredients into bowl. With pastry blender or mixer, blend in lard and butter or margarine until pieces are size of small peas. Add just enough water to hold dough together. Turn onto floured surface and knead gently for a few seconds. Divide dough and roll each half into a 10-inch circle, flouring surface if needed. Bake according to recipe.

Sour Cream Apple Pie

INN AT STARLIGHT LAKE
Starlight, Pennsylvania

6 TO 8 SERVINGS

CRUST
  1 cup all purpose flour
  ¼ teaspoon salt
  ¼ cup (½ stick) butter, chilled
  ¼ cup ice water

FILLING
  1 cup sour cream
  ¾ cup sugar
  1 egg
  2 tablespoons flour
  1 teaspoon vanilla
  ¼ teaspoon freshly ground nutmeg
  ⅛ teaspoon salt
  2 cups peeled, diced or shredded tart apples

TOPPING
  ⅓ cup brown sugar
  ⅓ cup flour
  1 teaspoon cinnamon
  2 tablespoons (¼ stick) butter, melted

Preheat oven to 400°F.

FOR CRUST: In mixing bowl, combine flour and salt. Add butter to flour, blending until mixture is texture of coarse meal. Add ice water all at once and stir until dough holds together and forms a ball leaving side of bowl clean. Roll into a 10-inch circle on lightly floured surface. Butter 9-inch pie plate and line with dough.

FOR FILLING: In bowl, combine sour cream, sugar, egg, flour, vanilla, nutmeg and salt. Blend well. Stir in apples and pour into unbaked pie crust. Bake 15 minutes in lower third of oven, then reduce heat to 350°F and bake until apples are tender, about 25 to 30 minutes longer. Remove pie from oven. Retain oven temperature at 350°F.

FOR TOPPING: In clean bowl, combine brown sugar, flour and cinnamon. Pour in melted butter and toss with fork until mixture is crumbly. Sprinkle over top of pie and bake until lightly browned, about 10 minutes.

Fruit pies, served hot or cold and using locally grown produce, are always popular. Tart apples make the best apple pie and can be mixed with sour cream to produce the delicious pie from the Inn at Starlight Lake in Pennsylvania. Latticed Cherry Pie as baked at the Kendron Valley Inn, South Woodstock, Vermont, attractively allows a glimpse of the luscious red fruit. Berries can be cooked, as in the Deep Dish Strawberry and Apple Pie baked at the Black Bass Inn, Lumberville, Pennsylvania, or uncooked, as in the famed Raspberry Tart from the Shandanken Inn in New York or the glazed Strawberry Tart prepared at L'Hostellerie Bressane.

Yadvigo's Cheese Pie

PILGRIM'S INN
Deer Isle, Maine

8 TO 10 SERVINGS

- 1 pound cream cheese, room temperature
- 3 eggs
- 1 cup sugar
- ½ cup sour cream
- 2 tablespoons powdered sugar
- 1 tablespoon vanilla
  Strawberries (optional)

Preheat oven to 325°F. Blend cream cheese, eggs and sugar in food processor or beat until smooth by hand. Pour into 9-inch pie dish and bake until tester inserted in center comes out clean, about 45 minutes. Cool 15 minutes.

In small bowl, mix sour cream, powdered sugar and vanilla. Pour mixture over cooled cheese pie. Return to oven until top is nicely set but not browned, about 15 minutes. Serve plain or decorate with fresh strawberries.

David's Cheesecake

WHEATLEIGH
Lenox, Massachusetts

6 TO 8 SERVINGS

CRUST

- 1 cup flour
- ½ cup brown sugar, tightly packed
- 1 cup finely ground walnuts
- ⅓ cup (¾ stick) butter, melted

FILLING

- 2 8-ounce packages cream cheese, room temperature
- ½ cup sugar
- 2 eggs
- 5 tablespoons whipping cream
- 2 teaspoons vanilla
  Juice of lemon

FOR CRUST: Preheat oven to 350°F. In large bowl, combine flour, brown sugar and walnuts. Stir in butter. Mix with hands until consistency of dough is light and crumbly. Reserve ½ cup of mixture to be used as topping. Place remainder of dough in 9-inch deep-dish pie pan or springform pan, pressing firmly to cover bottom and sides. Cover with aluminum foil weighed down with beans. Bake until crust is set and lightly brown, about 10 to 12 minutes. Remove beans and foil and allow center to dry in oven for at least 3 minutes. Remove from oven and allow to cool.

FOR FILLING: In large bowl with electric mixer, beat cream cheese with sugar until smooth. Beat in eggs, cream, vanilla and lemon juice, blending well. Pour mixture into crust. Sprinkle with reserve dough crumbs. Return to oven and bake until edge of cheesecake becomes golden brown, about 20 to 25 minutes. Refrigerate at least 3 to 4 hours before serving.

L'HOSTELLERIE BRESSANE

Jean Morel, chef and owner of L'Hostellerie Bressane, is bringing distinctive French cuisine to new heights in upstate Hillsdale, New York. Among other honors, he was recently named a master chef of France by the prestigious L'Association des Maîtres Cuisinier de France. Guests stay here to make sure they will get a dinner reservation.

152 Latticed Cherry Pie

KEDRON VALLEY INN
South Woodstock, Vermont

6 SERVINGS

PIECRUST
    Pastry for 9-inch 2-crust pie (*see page 176*)
1 tablespoon half and half

FILLING
1 16-ounce can cherry pie filling
¼ cup sugar
½ teaspoon cinnamon
1 tablespoon lemon juice
1 tablespoon butter, cut into small pieces

FOR PIECRUST: Make pastry, divide in half and form into 2 balls and flatten. Roll 1 ball out ⅛ inch thick on lightly floured board or pastry cloth. Fit into bottom of pie pan and trim ¼ inch beyond rim. Roll out remaining pastry ball into rectangle 10 inches long, ⅛ inch thick. Cut into at least sixteen ½-inch-wide strips.

FOR FILLING: Empty cherry pie filling into bowl and blend in sugar and cinnamon. Stir in lemon juice and butter. Pour evenly into pie pan. Lay 8 pastry strips across filling. Weave remaining strips over and under first strips, beginning at middle of pie and working first to one edge, then to other.

Preheat oven to 400°F. Trim strips to fit lower crust. Moisten rim with cold water and fold crust over strips. Press into a scalloped edge around pan and brush with half and half. Bake pie 30 minutes in lower third of oven. Reduce heat to 350°F and continue to bake until crust is nicely browned and filling bubbles in center, about 15 minutes.

Frozen Lemon Pie

PHILBROOK FARM INN
Shelburne, New Hampshire

6 TO 8 SERVINGS

This pie may be sprinkled with graham cracker crumbs before freezing, or topped with dabs of whipped cream when served.

CRUST
1 cup graham cracker crumbs
3 tablespoons (⅜ stick) butter, melted
3 tablespoons sugar
¼ teaspoon salt

FILLING
3 eggs, separated
½ cup plus 1 teaspoon sugar
    Juice and freshly grated zest of 1 large lemon
1 cup heavy cream

FOR CRUST: Preheat oven to 350°F. In mixing bowl, combine crumbs, butter, sugar and salt. Mix thoroughly. Pour mixture into 9-inch pie pan and press into shape using fingers or back of spoon. Bake for 10 minutes. Set aside.

FOR FILLING: In clean mixing bowl, beat egg yolks with ½ cup sugar until light. Blend in lemon juice and zest. Beat egg whites with remaining sugar until stiff but not dry. Fold into egg yolk mixture. Whip cream to stiff peaks and fold into mixture. Pour into graham cracker crust. Freeze at least 5 hours.

Raspberry Tart

SHANDAKEN INN
Shandaken, New York

6 TO 8 SERVINGS

PASTRY
2 cups flour
½ cup sugar
1 egg
¾ cup (1½ sticks) unsalted butter, cut in small pieces, room temperature
1 egg, beaten

FILLING
1 cup milk
2 tablespoons Cognac or California brandy
3 egg yolks
½ cup sugar
2 tablespoons cornstarch
2–3 pints fresh raspberries
2 teaspoons sugar

FOR PASTRY: In large bowl, place flour and make a well in center. Add sugar and whole egg. Begin blending with mixer or pastry blender. Add butter gradually. Continue blending until butter almost disappears. Knead dough 2 or 3 times. Form ball and wrap in towel or waxed paper. Refrigerate at least 1 hour but preferably 3 hours.

Preheat oven to 425°F. Roll out dough ⅛ inch thick and line 10-inch pie pan. Cover dough with waxed paper and fill with about 1½ cups uncooked rice. Bake until dough is completely set and beginning to brown, about 25 minutes. Remove paper and rice. Brush crust with some of beaten egg and continue baking until entire crust is lightly browned, about 5 minutes longer. Let cool.

Jean's "Adventures in Cooking" seminars, conducted at the inn, are liberally sprinkled with culinary advice. Among the most important: "Taste, taste, taste, and taste. You must taste the food. You read that something must simmer for half an hour. That is nonsense. You must taste it. That will tell you when it is ready. Taste is everything."

Strawberry Tart

L'HOSTELLERIE BRESSANE
Hillsdale, New York

8 SERVINGS

1 pint medium strawberries

SUGAR DOUGH
    1 cup all purpose flour, sifted
    ¼ cup superfine sugar
    ½ teaspoon salt
    ⅓ cup shortening
    2 tablespoons cold water

PASTRY CREAM
    2 cups milk
    1 teaspoon vanilla
    ½ cup plus 2 tablespoons sugar
    ¼ cup flour
    4 egg yolks
    1 whole egg
    1 tablespoon butter
      Grand Marnier to taste

GLAZE
    ½ cup strawberry jam
      Water to thin

Clean and hull the strawberries; then set aside.

FOR SUGAR DOUGH: In medium bowl, combine flour, sugar and salt. Remove ¼ cup of mixture; set aside. With pastry blender or two knives, cut in shortening until mixture is texture of coarse meal. Make a paste of reserved flour mixture and water; sprinkle over flour-shortening mixture. Using a fork, quickly blend together until flour is moistened and can be made into a ball. Refrigerate at least 2 hours. When ready to use, preheat oven to 400°F. Roll out dough on lightly floured board to ⅛-inch thickness. Line 9-inch pie plate. Prick bottom and sides thoroughly with fork. Bake until golden brown, about 8 to 10 minutes. Remove from oven and allow to cool.

FOR PASTRY CREAM: In 4-quart saucepan, bring milk and vanilla to boil. In large bowl, combine sugar and flour; make a well in center. Drop egg yolks and egg into well and gradually beat into flour mixture with wire whisk. When thoroughly mixed, add boiled milk slowly, whisking constantly. When blended and smooth, return entire mixture to saucepan and bring to boil over medium heat, whisking until cream is thick. Pour into large bowl and dot with butter. When cool, cover and refrigerate. When ready to fill shell, add Grand Marnier to taste, mix well and turn into prepared pastry shell. Top pastry cream with strawberries, stem end down, starting at rim and filling tart. Glaze tart with warm strawberry glaze, then refrigerate.

FOR GLAZE: In 1-cup saucepan, heat jam over low heat until warm and melting, adding just enough water to achieve proper consistency.

FOR FILLING: In 1-quart saucepan, bring milk and brandy to boil; set aside. In blender or with electric beater, blend yolks, ½ cup sugar and cornstarch until mixture is pale yellow. Slowly add hot milk and brandy, blending or whipping constantly. Return mixture to saucepan and bring to boil, beating or whisking constantly. Cook until mixture thickens, about 2 to 3 minutes. If lumpy, strain through sieve. Pour into bowl and cover surface with waxed paper to prevent skin from forming. Cool at least 30 minutes. Pour into tart shell. Cover generously with raspberries; sprinkle berries with remaining sugar. Run under broiler until berries are glazed, about 1 minute.

154 Deep Dish Strawberry and Apple Pie

BLACK BASS INN
Lumberville, Pennsylvania

4 TO 6 SERVINGS

CRUST
- ½ cup all purpose flour
- ½ cup whole wheat flour
- ½ teaspoon salt
- ½ cup solid vegetable shortening or lard, chilled
- 3 tablespoons ice water
- 1 tablespoon fresh lemon juice

FILLING
- 2–2½ tablespoons sugar
- 1½ tablespoons cornstarch
- 1 teaspoon cinnamon
- 4 large tart apples, peeled, cored and thinly sliced
- 1 pint strawberries, halved
- 1 tablespoon butter

FOR CRUST: In bowl, combine flours and salt. Cut in lard with pastry blender or 2 knives until mixture resembles coarse meal. Add water and lemon juice and mix with fork until dough leaves sides of bowl. Divide dough in half. Roll out one half and line 8 × 8-inch baking pan or 10-inch deep dish pie pan. Roll other half for top crust and set aside.

FOR FILLING: Preheat oven to 400°F. In 3-quart mixing bowl, combine sugar, cornstarch and cinnamon. Add apples and toss to coat evenly. Arrange half in lined pan. Layer with half of strawberries. Repeat with remaining apples, then remaining strawberries. Dot with butter. Cover with top crust and cut vents. Bake until crust is firm and lightly browned, about 30 minutes.

Marbled Chocolate Rum Pie

LOGAN INN
New Hope, Pennsylvania

8 TO 10 SERVINGS

FILLING
- ¾ cup sugar
- 1½ envelopes unflavored gelatin
- ⅛ teaspoon salt
- 2 egg yolks
- 1 cup milk
- 12 ounces semisweet chocolate bits
- 6 tablespoons dark Jamaican rum
- 2 egg whites
- 1 deep 9-inch piecrust, baked (see page 176)
- 1 cup whipping cream
- 1 teaspoon vanilla
- ¼ cup sugar

FOR FILLING: In top of double boiler over simmering water, mix ¼ cup sugar, gelatin and salt. Beat in egg yolks and milk. Cook, stirring constantly, until slightly thickened. Remove from heat and add chocolate, stirring until mixture is well blended. Remove top of double boiler and blend rum into mixture. Allow to cool, then chill until thickened but not set, about 20 minutes. Beat egg whites until foamy, gradually adding ½ cup sugar. Beat until stiff peaks form. Fold into chocolate mixture and spoon into crust.

Beat cream and vanilla briefly. Gradually add ¼ cup sugar. Continue beating until stiff. Drop 8 to 12 tablespoons whipped cream mixture onto top of filling. Using a spatula, stir through filling to make marble swirls. Chill pie until firm, at least 2 to 3 hours. Serve with remaining whipped cream.

Pecan Pie

WINDFLOWER INN
Great Barrington, Massachusetts

8 TO 10 SERVINGS

CRUST
- 1¾ cups flour
- 10 tablespoons (1¼ sticks) cold butter
- 2 tablespoons solid vegetable shortening
- ¼ teaspoon salt
  Pinch sugar
- ¼ cup ice-cold orange juice

FILLING
- ½ cup plus 2 tablespoons each light and dark corn syrup, combined
- 1 cup sugar
- 5 extra large eggs, beaten
- 6 tablespoons (¾ stick) butter, melted
- 2 tablespoons rum, preferably dark
- 1 teaspoon vanilla
- 2 cups chopped pecans

FOR CRUST: Put flour, butter, shortening, salt and sugar into food processor. Mix until ingredients are texture of coarse meal. Continue to mix, slowly adding juice, until dough forms a ball. Refrigerate about 1 hour. Roll out and line 10-inch pie plate. Refrigerate.

FOR FILLING: Preheat oven to 350°F. In 1-quart saucepan bring syrup and sugar to low boil and continue cooking until sugar is dissolved. Stir frequently. Remove from heat and beat into eggs. Stir in butter, rum and vanilla. Add pecans. Pour into pie shell and bake in lower third of oven until top looks crusty and a dull knife comes out clean when inserted midway between center and edge of filling, 50 minutes to 1 hour.

CHEESE AND FRUIT

Long traditional as the perfect finale after a heavy dinner, a selection of cheese and fruit is increasingly popular in these weight-conscious days. The San Ysidro Ranch at Montecito, California, serves an array of cheeses and fruits with their dessert buffet.

The French classics—Brie, Camembert and Roquefort—may be spread on thin slices of apples or pears. These fruits also combine well with semisoft cheeses. Berries are appropriate with creamy cheeses, and grapes mate with almost any variety. And for an unusual match, try Greek feta served cold with watermelon. Whatever the choice, the fruit must be unblemished and the cheese at its peak of perfection.

Mocha Tart

STONEHENGE
Ridgefield, Connecticut

---

6 TO 8 SERVINGS

CRUST
1½ cups sifted flour
  1 ounce unsweetened chocolate, finely ground
  ¾ cup finely ground walnuts
  ⅓ cup firmly packed dark brown sugar
  6 tablespoons (¾ stick) unsalted butter, melted
  1 egg
  1 tablespoon vanilla
  1 tablespoon cold water

FILLING
  1 ounce unsweetened chocolate, melted
  1 tablespoon instant coffee
  ½ cup plus 2 tablespoons (1¼ sticks) unsalted butter
  ¾ cup firmly packed dark brown sugar
  2 eggs, beaten

TOPPING
  1 cup whipping cream
  1 tablespoon instant coffee
  ¼ cup sugar

FOR CRUST: Preheat oven to 375°F. In large bowl, combine flour, chocolate, nuts and sugar. Make well in center. Beat butter, egg, vanilla and cold water together. Pour into well and blend with fork until dough leaves sides of bowl. Chill for ½ hour. Roll out ⅛ inch thick on lightly floured pastry cloth and line buttered 9-inch fluted pie plate. Cover with waxed paper and weigh down with rice or beans. Bake until set and slightly brown on the edges, about 20 minutes. Remove paper and rice and return to oven to lightly brown, about 5 minutes. Set aside to cool.

FOR FILLING: In top of double boiler, melt chocolate and coffee together. Set aside to cool. In medium bowl, cream butter. Add sugar 2 tablespoons at a time, beating well after each addition until light and fluffy. Add eggs 2 tablespoons at a time, beating well after each addition. Mixture should hold peaks and be fluffy. Fold in chocolate and coffee mixture. Pour into cooled pie shell and chill.

FOR TOPPING: In medium bowl, mix coffee in cream and beat in sugar 2 tablespoons at a time. Continue beating until cream is stiff. Spread over filling and finish by swirling topping with back of spoon.

Grammy Bowles' Maple Sugar Cake

THE HOMESTEAD
Sugar Hill, New Hampshire

---

6 TO 8 SERVINGS
  1 egg yolk
  1 cup soft maple sugar (or 1 cup light brown sugar well mixed with 2 teaspoons maple flavoring)
  1 cup sour cream
  1 teaspoon baking soda
  1 teaspoon salt
  ½ teaspoon (scant) warm water
1½–2 cups flour
  1 egg white
  1 cup chopped walnuts (or butternuts, if available)
  1 teaspoon maple flavoring (optional)

Preheat oven to 350°F. In large mixing bowl, beat egg yolk well and beat in sugar. Stir in sour cream. In small bowl, dissolve baking soda and salt in water to make a paste and blend into mixture. Blend in flour starting with 1½ cups and adding extra ½ cup if needed. In small mixing bowl, beat egg white until stiff but not dry and fold into flour mixture along with nuts. If desired, add maple flavoring for stronger taste. Bake in greased 9 × 9-inch pan until toothpick inserted in center comes out clean, about 40 minutes.

SQUIRE TARBOX INN

Ann McInvale, one of the innkeepers of the Squire Tarbox Inn, Wiscasset, Maine, does most of the cooking in the commodious kitchen. From elegant cream soups to exotic desserts, her excellent cooking is prepared with a fine Southern hand. A Southern Poppyseed Dressing and the fabulous Sin Pie are two of her recipes included in this collection.

156 # Sin Pie

Ross's Chocolate Cake

SQUIRE TARBOX INN
Wiscasset, Maine

6 TO 8 SERVINGS

CRUST
- 1 cup graham cracker crumbs
- 2 tablespoons sugar
- 3 tablespoons (⅜ stick) butter, melted

FILLING
- 1½ cups powdered sugar
- ½ cup plus 2 tablespoons (1¼ sticks) unsalted butter, room temperature
- 2 extra large eggs, beaten
- 1 teaspoon white crème de menthe
- 4 ounces semisweet chocolate, melted
  Whipped cream (garnish)
  Slivered almonds (garnish)

FOR CRUST: Preheat oven to 375°F. In bowl, combine graham cracker crumbs and sugar. Add butter, blending well with fork. Press into bottom and sides of 8-inch pie pan. Bake until lightly brown and set, about 8 to 10 minutes. Cool on rack.

FOR FILLING: Beat sugar and butter until mixture is like stiff whipped cream, about 5 to 6 minutes. Gradually add eggs, beating well after each addition. Blend in liqueur, then melted chocolate. Pour into cooled pie shell and chill immediately. When ready to serve, top with the whipped cream and almonds.

KILMUIR PLACE
Cape Breton, Nova Scotia, Canada

8 TO 10 SERVINGS

CAKE
- 1 cup shortening
- 2 cups sugar
- 4 1-ounce squares unsweetened chocolate, melted
- 5 eggs
- 2 teaspoons vanilla
- 2¼ cups cake flour, sifted
- 1 teaspoon baking soda
- 1 teaspoon salt
- 1 cup buttermilk or sour milk

FROSTING
- 2 cups powdered sugar
- ½ cup (1 stick) margarine, room temperature
- ½ cup milk
- ⅓ cup cocoa
- ¼ teaspoon salt
- 1 teaspoon vanilla

FOR CAKE: Preheat oven to 350°F. In large bowl with electric mixer, cream together shortening and sugar. Add chocolate, eggs and vanilla and blend well. In medium bowl, sift together flour, baking soda and salt. Add to creamed mixture alternately with buttermilk, beginning and ending with dry ingredients, and beat until smooth. Pour batter into 2 greased 9-inch layer cake pans and bake until tester comes out clean, about 40 minutes. Remove from oven, invert onto cake rack and cool.

FOR FROSTING: In a 1½-quart saucepan, combine powdered sugar, margarine, milk, cocoa and salt. Bring to rolling boil and continue to boil for 2 minutes stirring constantly. Remove from heat and cool. Add vanilla and beat until smooth-spreading consistency is achieved. Spread layer of frosting over top of one cake. Fit second cake carefully on frosted top. Frost top and sides of layer cake.

RIGHT:
Ross's Chocolate Cake (top) from Kilmuir Place and Sin Pie (bottom) from Squire Tarbox Inn illustrate the two recipes on this page.

Mocha Tart, bottom right, is one of a number of superb desserts served at Stonehenge, Ridgefield, Connecticut. *See page 155.*

Carrot Cake from the Wayside Inn, Middletown, Virginia. *See page* 165.

Strawberry Hazelnut Torte from the Copper Beech Inn, Ivoryton, Connecticut. *See page* 168.

RIGHT:
Salishan English Trifle
shown in the glorious setting
of the dining room at
Salishan Lodge,
Gleneden Beach, Oregon.
See page 167.

A variety of cheeses are offered for dessert, along with fruit,
at San Ysidro Ranch, Montecito, California.
For a further discussion of the merits of cheese and fruit at
dessert time, *see page* 155.

RIGHT:
Zabaglione is an Italian
dessert that is a specialty at
The Elms, Ridgefield,
Connecticut.
See page 172.

LEFT:
Grand Marnier Mousse
in Swans is the
most exotic dessert
served at the
Copper Beech Inn,
Ivoryton, Connecticut.
See page 174.

A SPECIAL TREAT

The Bee and Thistle Inn, Old Lyme, Connecticut, is noted for serving breakfast in bed to guests still recovering from the previous evening's feasting. A simple tray of muffins, fruit and coffee usually suffices.

Carrot Cake

Yogurt Cake with Orange Glaze

WAYSIDE INN
Middletown, Virginia

8 TO 10 SERVINGS

CAKE
- 2⅓ cups cake flour (or 2 cups plus 1 tablespoon all purpose flour)
- 2 cups sugar
- 2 teaspoons baking powder
- 2 teaspoons cinnamon
- 1 teaspoon baking soda
- 1 teaspoon salt
- 1¼ cups salad oil
- 4 eggs
- 2 teaspoons vanilla
- 2 cups grated carrots
- ½ cup chopped pecans

ICING
- 2 3-ounce packages cream cheese, room temperature
- 3 tablespoons whipping cream
- 1½ teaspoons vanilla
- ½ teaspoon salt
- 1 1-pound box powdered sugar
- ¾ cup chopped pecans
- ½ cup coconut

FOR CAKE: Preheat oven to 325°F. Grease and flour 2 round 9-inch cake pans; set aside. Sift together flour, sugar, baking powder, cinnamon, baking soda and salt into large bowl of electric mixer. Add oil and beat 2 minutes, starting at medium speed, increasing to high and scraping sides of bowl several times. Add eggs and vanilla and beat 2 minutes more, scraping sides of bowl. Stir in carrots

and pecans. Divide batter between pans. Bake until tester inserted into center of cake comes out clean, about 40 to 50 minutes. Let cool 15 minutes in pan, then turn out onto rack to cool completely.

FOR ICING: In small bowl, combine cream cheese, cream, vanilla and salt and beat until consistency of very soft paste, about 5 to 7 minutes. Gradually add sugar 1 cup at a time, blending well after each addition. Stir in pecans and coconut. Spread icing over top (not sides) of each cake. Transfer to serving plate.

BEE AND THISTLE INN
Old Lyme, Connecticut

8 SERVINGS

CAKE
- 2½ cups sifted flour
- ½ teaspoon baking soda
- ½ teaspoon salt
- ¾ cup (1½ sticks) butter, room temperature
- 1½ cups sugar
- 3 eggs
- 1 teaspoon vanilla
- 1 teaspoon freshly grated lemon peel
- 1½ cups yogurt (do not exceed)

GLAZE
- 2 tablespoons (¼ stick) butter, room temperature
- 1½ cups sifted powdered sugar
- 1 tablespoon grated orange or lemon zest
- ½ teaspoon orange or lemon extract
- 2–3 tablespoons cream (optional)

Preheat oven to 325°F. Butter and lightly flour an angel food cake pan.
FOR CAKE: Sift together flour, baking soda and salt. In mixing bowl, cream butter until soft and continue to beat while gradually adding sugar until mixture is light and creamy. In separate bowl, combine eggs, vanilla and lemon peel. Beat well about 15 seconds. Slowly add to butter mixture in 4 to 5 steps, beating continuously until completely absorbed and mixture is pale yellow and quite fluffy. Fold flour and yogurt alternately into batter, in 2 steps each. Pour into cake pan. Bake until tooth-

Chocolate Decadence

ST. ORRES
Gualala, California

12 SERVINGS

Prepare one day in advance.

1¼ pounds dark sweet chocolate
½ cup plus 2 tablespoons (1¼ sticks) unsalted butter
5 eggs
1 tablespoon sugar
1 tablespoon flour

1¼ cups whipping cream
2 tablespoons powdered sugar
2 tablespoons orange liqueur
1 10-ounce package frozen raspberries, thawed

Preheat oven to 425°F. In 1-quart double boiler, melt 1 pound chocolate with butter; set aside. In large metal bowl, combine eggs and sugar. Place bowl over pan of boiling water. Using wire whisk, beat sugar and eggs until sugar dissolves and mixture is warm to touch. With electric mixer, immediately beat mixture until triple in volume, about 5 to 10 minutes. Fold flour and chocolate mixture into egg mixture. Pour into 8-inch round cake pan lined with parchment paper. Bake exactly 15 minutes and allow to cool. Place in freezer for at least 24 hours.

pick or wire tester comes out clean, 80 to 90 minutes. Cool on rack.

FOR ICING: Cream butter until soft and continue beating, gradually adding sugar, until light and creamy. Beat in peel and extract. Beat in cream, if desired, 1 tablespoon at a time until glaze reaches spreadable consistency. Glaze cake.

When ready to serve, remove cake from pan and peel off paper. Place on serving plate. Whip cream with powdered sugar and orange liqueur until peaks form. Top cake with whipped cream mixture, reserving some for piping through pastry bag to make rosette decorations around top rim. With potato peeler, form curls from remaining chocolate and pile curls in center of whipped cream topping. Puree raspberries in blender and sieve out seeds. Allow cake to sit at room temperature for 30 minutes before serving. Serve with raspberry puree.

The English trifle at left and in the color photograph on page 173 was taken in the Gourmet Dining Room at Salishan Lodge, Gleneden Beach, Oregon. The dining room has an international reputation, and is an imposing room built on three levels and finished in natural woods, with windows all around that allow diners to enjoy the rugged view. Although seafood is the specialty, the menu is nine pages long, and if given 48 hours notice, Chef Franz Buck can prepare dishes from the cuisines of virtually any country.

Salishan
English Trifle

SALISHAN LODGE
Gleneden Beach, Oregon

10 TO 12 SERVINGS

SPONGE CAKE JELLY ROLL
- 6 eggs, separated (room temperature or slightly warmer)
- 1 cup sugar
- 1 tablespoon warm water
  Pinch salt
- 1 cup all purpose flour sifted 3 times with 1 teaspoon baking powder
- 1 12-ounce jar raspberry preserves

SYRUP
- 2 cups water
- 2 cups sugar
- 2 cups good quality rum, or 1 cup rum mixed with 1 cup sherry

TRIFLE
- 1 pound shelled almonds, hazelnuts or macadamian nuts, coarsely chopped or slivered
- 1 12-ounce package chocolate chips
- 1 15-ounce box raisins
- 2 cups heavy whipped cream*
- 12–16 macaroons (optional)
  Maraschino cherries (garnish)
  Fresh mint sprigs (garnish)
  Candied angelica (optional garnish)

FOR SPONGE CAKE JELLY ROLL: Line 18 × 12-inch jelly roll pan or 2 small jelly roll pans with waxed paper; set aside. Preheat oven to 350°F. In large bowl, beat egg yolks, sugar and water until thick and pale yellow. In medium bowl, beat egg whites with salt until stiff glossy peaks form. With rubber spatula, slip egg whites to rest atop beaten egg yolks. Gradually add flour and baking powder combination and gently fold into egg whites and yolks. Batter may look streaky, but do not mix too thoroughly; it must be light and fluffy. Pour batter into pan and level to fill corners. Bake until golden brown and cake tester inserted in center comes out clean, about 20 minutes for 1 pan, 15 minutes for 2. Remove from oven immediately and turn upside down on large tea towel or two layers of cheesecloth larger than pan. While cake is still hot, remove waxed paper. If it sticks, brush outside with cold water. Trim off hard or crusty edges. Spread preserves evenly over top of cake and roll tightly. Wrap roll in tea towel or cheesecloth; waxed paper may be used if jelly roll has cooled to room temperature. Refrigerate at least 3 hours.

FOR SYRUP: In 2-quart saucepan, bring water and sugar to boil, stirring until sugar dissolves. Cool. Add rum or rum and sherry; mix well.

FOR TRIFLE: Remove refrigerated jelly roll from cloth and slice into ¾-inch slices. Line bottom then sides of 10- to 12-inch serving bowl using nicest slices for outside layer. Sprinkle slices evenly with nuts, chocolate chips and raisins; bind to cake with whipped cream. Fill bowl with alternating layers of cake, nuts, chocolate chips, raisins and whipped cream. Level bowl with end cuts and trimmings of jelly roll, or macaroons if desired. Slowly pour about third of syrup over full bowl allowing time for trifle to absorb syrup. Repeat until all syrup is completely absorbed. Chill thoroughly, preferably 24 hours but no less than 6. When ready to serve, turn bowl upside down on serving platter, tapping pan with back of knife if necessary to release trifle from bowl. It should be dome shaped. Decorate with whipped cream, maraschino cherries, mint leaves, candied angelica, chocolate chips and nuts.

* Vanilla pudding may be combined with whipped cream or used instead of whipped cream.

168 Strawberry Hazelnut Torte

Lime Dacquoise

COPPER BEECH INN
Ivoryton, Connecticut

10 SERVINGS

TORTE

    8 egg whites, room temperature
    2 cups sugar
 1½ cups finely ground roasted
      hazelnuts
      Butter (optional)
      Cornstarch (optional)

FILLING

    4 pints rinsed fresh strawberries,
      hulled and blotted dry
      Sugar
    1 quart heavy cream
    6 tablespoons powdered sugar
  ¼ cup Grand Marnier
    1 10–12-ounce jar raspberry
      preserves
   10 fresh mint leaves (optional
      garnish)

FOR TORTE: Preheat oven to 200°F. In large bowl using electric mixer, beat egg whites until soft peaks form, about 3 to 5 minutes. Gradually add sugar, beating continuously until all sugar is dissolved and egg whites form stiff glossy peaks, about 15 to 20 minutes. Fold hazelnuts into egg whites. Spoon into pastry bag and pipe out three 9-inch diameter ½-inch-high meringue discs onto baking sheet lined with parchment paper or brown paper buttered and lightly dusted with cornstarch. Smooth meringues. Bake until very lightly browned and firm to touch, about 1 to 1½ hours. Let cool on wire racks in dry place or dry in oven with heat turned off and door ajar.

FOR FILLING: Reserve enough whole strawberries of uniform size to top one 9-inch disc. In shallow broiler pan, place whole strawberries and sprinkle with sugar. Place under broiler for 1 minute to glaze; set aside. Thinly slice remaining strawberries and place in large bowl; set aside. In large bowl, combine cream and powdered sugar. Whip until almost stiff. Add Grand Marnier and continue whipping until stiff. Spread one-third raspberry preserves over each meringue. Cover each with layer of sliced strawberries, using one-third per layer. Cover two discs with whipped cream leaving third disc for top of torte. Carefully stack meringue discs in layers. Cover top disc with whipped cream. Decorate top with glazed whole strawberries. Cover sides of torte with remaining whipped cream. If desired, decorate with rosettes of whipped cream and mint leaves.

1770 HOUSE
East Hampton, New York

8 TO 10 SERVINGS

MERINGUE

    1 cup (8–10) egg whites
  ½ teaspoon cream of tartar
    4 tablespoons sugar
    1 teaspoon vanilla
  ½ teaspoon almond extract
 1½ tablespoons cornstarch
 1⅓ cups ground almonds
    1 cup sugar

FILLING

  ¾ cup sugar
    4 whole eggs
    6 egg yolks
      Juice and peel of 5 limes
    1 teaspoon butter

    1 cup whipping cream, whipped

FOR MERINGUE: Preheat oven to 375°F. In medium mixing bowl with electric mixer, beat egg whites with cream of tartar until they form thick glossy mounds but are not dry. Gradually beat in 4 tablespoons sugar, 1 tablespoon at a time, mixing well after each addition. Add vanilla and almond extract and beat a few minutes longer. Fold cornstarch and ground almonds into meringue mixture. Sift remaining 1 cup sugar over mixture and fold in. Fill pastry bag with mixture and pipe out three 9-inch solid circles, like thin flat cakes, on greased and floured baking sheets. Reduce oven to 275°F and bake until firm but uncolored, about

AN EVENING RITUAL

Hot chocolate and homemade gingersnaps are an evening ritual at the Marshlands Inn, Sackville, New Brunswick. This wonderful combination allays the guests' nocturnal cravings while warming them up for a peaceful slumber.

Gingersnaps

Pecan Crunch

60 to 70 minutes. Remove to rack and allow to cool and dry before filling.

FOR FILLING: In 1-quart saucepan, combine sugar, eggs, egg yolks, lime juice and peel. Cook over moderate heat, stirring constantly, until very thick. Remove from heat and swirl in butter; let cool.

TO ASSEMBLE: Place one meringue layer on cake turntable or serving dish; spread with lime mixture. Repeat, ending with lime. Decorate with whipped cream, allowing lime layers to show through.

THE MARSHLANDS INN
Sackville, New Brunswick, Canada

MAKES 3 TO 4 DOZEN

2½ cups all purpose flour
1½ teaspoons baking soda
½ teaspoon salt
½ cup chicken fat, melted, or shortening
¼ cup sugar
¾ cup molasses
1½ teaspoons ground ginger

In a bowl, sift together flour, baking soda and salt; set aside. In mixing bowl, combine chicken fat or shortening with sugar. Stir in molasses and ginger. Add flour mixture and blend until mixture holds together as soft, not sticky dough. Shape into 3 logs about 2 inches in diameter. Wrap logs in waxed paper and refrigerate 3 to 4 hours.

Preheat oven to 350°F. Grease three 11 × 16-inch cookie sheets. Remove waxed paper from dough and slice logs while cold into ⅛-inch-thick discs. Place discs on cookie sheets and bake until crisp and firm when touched with toothpick or finger, about 8 to 10 minutes. Remove from cookie sheets and cool on wire racks.

BLACK BASS HOTEL
Lumberville, Pennsylvania

6 TO 8 SERVINGS

6 egg whites, room temperature
⅛ teaspoon cream of tartar
Pinch salt
1 cup sugar
1 tablespoon baking powder
¼ teaspoon vanilla extract
3 cups pecans, coarsely chopped and toasted

Preheat oven to 375°F. Spray inside of 13 × 9 × 2-inch baking pan with nonstick cooking lubricant or line pan with cooking parchment and set aside. Place egg whites in mixing bowl, add cream of tartar and salt. Beat till soft peaks form. Continue beating and gradually add sugar 1 to 2 tablespoons at a time until mixture forms stiff glossy peaks. Fold in baking powder, vanilla extract and pecans. Spread mixture evenly in pan and bake until golden brown, about 10 minutes. Reduce heat to 300°F and continue baking until firm when pressed lightly with finger, about 15 to 30 minutes. Remove from pan and cool on rack. Meringue should be firm on all sides and semisoft inside.

170 Bananas Foster

Salade de Bananes au Kirsch

Pureed Fresh Fruit Sauce

CLIFF PARK INN
Milford, Pennsylvania

4 SERVINGS

¾ tablespoon butter
4 firm bananas, halved crosswise and lengthwise
3 tablespoons dark rum
1¼ tablespoons (approximate) banana liqueur
   Dash cinnamon to taste
4 scoops vanilla ice cream

Over medium to high heat, place sauté pan or chafing dish blazer and melt butter. Add bananas and cook until bananas are hot, about 1 or 2 minutes, turning occasionally with large spoon. Add 1 tablespoon rum, banana liqueur and cinnamon. Cook until bananas are heated but not soft, about 1 minute, scraping liquid from pan surfaces and basting bananas. Heat and ignite remaining 2 tablespoons of rum and pour over bananas. When flame dies, surround ice cream with bananas, pour the sauce over and serve.

L'HOSTELLERIE BRESSANE
Hillsdale, New York

4 TO 6 SERVINGS

   Zest of 1 orange, cut julienne
2 teaspoons sugar
3 ripe but firm bananas sliced in ¼–½-inch-thick rounds
   Juice of ½ orange
   Juice of ½ lemon
3 tablespoons kirsch

Combine orange peel and sugar in 2-cup saucepan with enough water to cover. Cook mixture over medium heat, shaking pan until sugar dissolves, then cook without stirring until almost caramelized. Remove from heat.

In medium bowl, carefully toss bananas with orange and lemon juices and kirsch until well combined. Gently stir in caramelized peel. Cover and refrigerate at least 2 hours before serving.

PUMP HOUSE INN
Canadensis, Pennsylvania

8 SERVINGS

12 strawberries, cleaned and hulled
   Juice of 1 orange
   Juice of 1 lemon
   Juice of 1 lime
½ cup cubed honeydew or cantaloupe
½ cup white seedless grapes
6 tablespoons Triple Sec
6 tablespoons honey
   Grated zest of 1 orange
   Grated zest of 1 lemon
   Grated zest of 1 lime

Combine strawberries, orange, lemon and lime juices, melon cubes, grapes, Triple Sec and honey together in blender or processor and puree for 10 seconds. Pour into medium bowl and stir in zests of orange, lemon and lime.

Serve cold or warm over strawberries or baked custard.

The photograph opposite, showing the preparation of Bananas Foster, was taken at tableside at the Cliff Park Inn in Milford, Pennsylvania, where food and golf are the main preoccupations. The inn is surrounded by a golf course and was originally used to accommodate private guests of the Buchanan family, who moved to the area in 1800. The inn has remained in the family, and Harry Buchanan, the present owner, continues to run it in the easygoing manner of an early country club.

Apple Spice Pudding

KILMUIR PLACE
Cape Breton, Nova Scotia, Canada

4 TO 6 SERVINGS

 2 cups peeled chopped apples
 1 cup flour
 1 cup sugar
 ¼ cup shortening
 1 egg
 1 teaspoon baking soda
 1 teaspoon cinnamon
 1 teaspoon cloves
 1 teaspoon nutmeg
 ½ cup whipping cream, whipped (garnish)

In large bowl, combine apples, flour, sugar, shortening, egg, baking soda, cinnamon, cloves and nutmeg; blend well. Pour into greased 8-inch square baking pan and bake until knife inserted between center and edge of pudding comes out clean, about 45 minutes. Serve warm topped with whipped cream.

Bread Pudding

TANQUE VERDE RANCH
Tucson, Arizona

8 TO 10 SERVINGS

SYRUP
 1 cup firmly packed brown sugar
 1 cup water
 1 cinnamon stick

PUDDING
  Butter
 ¾ cup raisins
 ½ pound French bread cut in ½-inch-thick slices, toasted
 ½ cup toasted pine nuts
 ½ cup toasted slivered almonds
 ½ cup toasted chopped walnuts
 ½ pound Monterey Jack cheese, cut in ½-inch cubes
 1 tart apple, peeled, cored and thinly sliced

  Whipped cream, ice cream or heavy cream (garnish)

FOR SYRUP: In 3-cup saucepan, combine all ingredients and boil until sugar is dissolved and syrup is slightly thickened, about 5 minutes. Discard cinnamon stick; set aside.

FOR PUDDING: Preheat oven to 350°F. Butter 9 × 13-inch baking dish; set aside. Reserve ¼ cup raisins. Break bread into large pieces and layer half on bottom of baking dish. In layers, add half of pine nuts, almonds, walnuts, raisins, cheese and apple. Cover with half syrup. Repeat layers. Top with reserved raisins and remaining syrup. Cover with foil and bake for 15 minutes. Uncover and bake until top is lightly browned, about 15 minutes. Serve warm with garnish.

Cranberry Pudding

171

KILMUIR PLACE
Cape Breton, Nova Scotia, Canada

6 SERVINGS

PUDDING
 ½ cup dark molasses
 2 teaspoons baking soda
 1⅓ cups flour
 1 cup cranberries
 ⅓ cup boiling water
 1 teaspoon baking powder

SAUCE
 ½ cup sugar
 ½ cup half and half
 ¼ cup (½ stick) butter, room temperature
 2 teaspoons rum
  Pinch salt

FOR PUDDING: Grease 1-quart pudding mold; set aside. In large bowl, combine molasses and baking soda. Add flour, cranberries, boiling water and baking powder and mix well. Pour into pudding mold. Cover tightly with foil and place on rack in large kettle. Add boiling water to come halfway up side of mold. Cover kettle and steam for 1 hour. Remove pudding from mold onto serving plate and serve hot with sauce.

FOR SAUCE: In 2-cup saucepan, mix together sugar, half and half, butter, rum and salt and bring to boil. Cool before pouring over the pudding.

172 Indian Pudding

THE HOMESTEAD
Sugar Hill, New Hampshire

8 TO 10 SERVINGS

In the old days this was served with heavy "pour" cream. It is equally good served with a scoop of vanilla ice cream.

1½ quarts (6 cups) milk
½ cup yellow cornmeal
2 cups cold milk
⅓ cup (scant ¾ stick) butter, room temperature
1 cup dark molasses
½ cup sugar
2 teaspoons salt
2 teaspoons ginger
¼ teaspoon cinnamon

Preheat oven to 300°F. Butter 9 × 13-inch baking dish, set aside. In 3-quart double boiler, scald 1½ quarts milk. In small bowl, make paste of cornmeal and ½ cup cold milk. Add to scalded milk. With wire whisk, stir in butter, molasses, sugar, salt, ginger and cinnamon until smooth and free of lumps. Pour into baking dish. Gently pour remaining 1½ cups cold milk evenly over top, taking care not to make a hole in center. Bake until knife inserted in center of pudding comes out clean, about 3 hours.

Zabaglione

THE ELMS
Ridgefield, Connecticut

2 SERVINGS

¼ cup sugar
2 egg yolks
1 tablespoon white wine
1 tablespoon sherry
Strawberries (garnish)

With wire whisk, beat sugar and egg yolks in top of 2-cup double boiler or heatproof bowl with round bottom over hot water, until mixture is creamy and foamy. Continue whisking while gradually adding wine and sherry in steady trickle. Beat until mixture swells and forms soft mounds. Spoon into tall stemmed glasses. Garnish with strawberries and serve immediately.

Crème de Menthe Parfait

TAUGHANNOCK FARMS INN
Trumansburg, New York

FOR EACH SERVING

2 tablespoons crème de menthe
1 scoop vanilla ice cream, slightly softened
1 scoop chocolate ice cream
Whipped cream and cherry (garnish)

Pour crème de menthe into bottom of parfait glass. Squeeze vanilla ice cream through pastry bag so ice cream is coiled into parfait glass. Add chocolate ice cream and top with whipped cream and cherry.

Cranberry Ice Burgundy

CHALET SUZANNE
Lake Wales, Florida

8 SERVINGS

This dish can be served as an accompaniment to meat.

1 tablespoon (1 envelope) unflavored gelatin
1½ cups bottled cranberry juice cocktail
1 cup sugar
¾ cup Burgundy
¼ cup orange juice
1 tablespoon lemon juice

In small bowl, dissolve gelatin in ¼ cup cranberry juice. In 1-quart saucepan, combine remaining cranberry juice, dissolved gelatin and sugar. Bring to boil and simmer for 5 minutes. Cool to room temperature. Stir in Burgundy, orange juice and lemon juice. Pour into ice cube tray and freeze until firm, at least 2 hours. For dessert, remove from freezer and beat with electric beater until frothy. Refreeze until ready to serve. Ice may be scraped out with soup spoon or portioned with ice cream scoop.

The Créme de Menthe Parfait from
Taughannock Farms Inn.

Toasted Almond-Coffee Ice Cream

SIGN OF THE SORREL HORSE
Quakertown, Pennsylvania

MAKES ½ GALLON

    2 cups milk
    8 egg yolks
    ¾ cup sugar
    ½ vanilla bean, split
    ⅛ teaspoon salt
    2 teaspoons instant coffee
    ¼ cup coffee
    1 quart (4 cups) whipping cream
    ¼ cup honey
    ½ cup coarsely ground toasted
       almonds

In top of 2-quart double boiler over simmering water, combine milk, egg yolks, sugar, vanilla bean and salt. Cook, stirring constantly, until mixture thickens enough to coat a wooden spoon. Discard vanilla bean, and allow custard to cool. In small bowl, dissolve instant coffee in ¼ cup coffee; set aside. In large bowl, combine cream, honey and dissolved coffee. Stir in egg mixture and blend well. Pour into ice cream freezer and freeze, following manufacturer's instructions. When partially frozen, stir in almonds.

Apricot Sherbet

THE VICTORIAN
Whitinsville, Massachusetts

10 SERVINGS

This recipe works equally well with fresh strawberries and strawberry jam, with raspberries and raspberry jam, or even with cantaloupe, providing someone has made cantaloupe jam!

    3 cups apricot jam
    1 pound apricots, canned or fresh (if
       fresh, should be fully ripe)
   1½ tablespoons lemon juice
    1 teaspoon vanilla
       Whipping cream (garnish)

In 1-quart saucepan, melt jam over low heat. Strain and discard solids. In blender or processor, puree apricots, strained jam, lemon juice and vanilla. Pour into large bowl and freeze until solid, about 4 to 6 hours. To serve, form into balls with ice cream scoop. Pour cream over top. Heavy cream is a must to enhance taste of sherbet.

Cold Chocolate Soufflé

COPPER BEECH
Ivoryton, Connecticut

4 SERVINGS

   1½ tablespoons (1½ envelopes) unfla-
       vored gelatin
    ¼ cup cold water
    2 teaspoons orange juice
   5½ ounces semisweet chocolate
    3 tablespoons strong coffee
    2 tablespoons brandy
    4 eggs
    3 egg yolks
    ½ cup sugar
    ½ cup whipping cream, whipped
    ½ cup whipped heavy cream (op-
       tional garnish)

In top of small double boiler over simmering water, dissolve gelatin in water and orange juice. Remove from heat; set aside. In small saucepan, melt chocolate in coffee and brandy; set aside. In large mixing bowl, combine eggs, egg yolks and sugar. Beat until very thick and pale in color, about 5 minutes. Add gelatin and chocolate mixture and mix well. Fold in whipping cream. Pour into 1-quart collared soufflé dish and refrigerate, preferably overnight. Remove collar and, if desired, garnish with whipped cream rosettes.

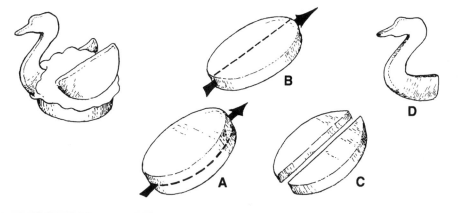

To make swans, cut a ⅜-inch-thick disc of pastry in half (A) after baking. One half is then cut in half again (B) to form wings (C). Spoon mousse onto the whole disc and insert neck (D) and wings to complete swan.

174 Cold Coffee Soufflé

L'HOSTELLERIE BRESSANE
Hillsdale, New York

10 SERVINGS

    2 cups strong coffee
 1¼ cups sugar
    1 cup water
  12 egg yolks
    1 quart (4 cups) whipping cream, whipped

In small saucepan, simmer coffee over low heat until light syrup forms, about 25 minutes. Meanwhile, in 1-quart saucepan, mix sugar and water and cook over low heat, stirring occasionally, until light syrup forms, about 25 minutes. In large mixing bowl, beat egg yolks with electric mixer until yolks form heavy ribbon. Stir sugar mixture slowly into egg yolks. Stir in coffee and cream. Beat very slowly for about 1 minute and then fold lightly by hand. Pour into individual ramekins and freeze for about 3 hours. Place in refrigerator about 30 minutes before serving.

Grand Marnier Mousse in Swans

COPPER BEECH INN
Ivoryton, Connecticut

6 SERVINGS

PASTRY SWANS
 ½ cup (scant) milk
2½ tablespoons butter
    Pinch salt
 ½ cup plus 2 tablespoons bread flour
  3 eggs

MOUSSE
 ¾ cup sugar
  4 eggs
  3 egg yolks
  2 tablespoons unflavored gelatin
 ⅓ cup Grand Marnier
1½ cups whipping cream
  1 teaspoon vanilla
    Powdered sugar, to taste

FOR PASTRY SWANS: Preheat oven to 400°F. In 1-quart saucepan, combine milk, butter and salt; bring to full boil. Remove from heat. Gradually mix in flour until pastry is smooth and rolls free from sides of pan. Beat in eggs, one at a time, until medium-stiff consistency. Shape into 6 separate "S" shape necks and 2-inch ovals for bodies. Place on greased sheet and bake 15 to 20 minutes.

FOR MOUSSE: In large bowl with electric mixer, beat sugar, eggs and yolks at high speed until eggs form thick ribbon, about 12 minutes. In top of small double boiler over simmering water, dissolve gelatin in Grand Marnier. Pour into egg mixture. Whip cream with vanilla; fold into mixture. Spoon into 6 pastry swan bodies, insert necks and top with sugar. Refrigerate 2 hours.

Maple Mousse

LYME INN
Lyme, New Hampshire

12 SERVINGS

    1 cup maple syrup
 ½ cup firmly packed light brown sugar
1½ tablespoons (1½ envelopes) unflavored gelatin, dissolved in ½ cup water
  4 egg yolks
  4 egg whites
  2 cups whipping cream, whipped

In 1-quart double boiler, combine maple syrup, brown sugar, dissolved gelatin and egg yolks over moderate heat and beat with wire whisk until stiff. Remove from heat, cool and allow to thicken slightly. In small mixing bowl, beat egg whites until stiff peaks form. Fold egg whites and whipped cream into syrup mixture. Pour into wide-bowl champagne glasses; refrigerate at least 2 hours.

BASIC RECIPES

Brown Sauce
(Demi-Glace)

MAKES 1 QUART

- 2 tablespoons (¼ stick) unsalted butter
- 1 medium onion, thinly sliced
- 1 medium carrot, diced
- 1 celery stalk (including leaves), thinly sliced
- 1 ounce prosciutto or other ham, diced
- ½ cup (1 stick) unsalted butter
- ½ cup all purpose flour
- 2 quarts degreased rich unsalted beef stock, heated to boiling
- 10 parsley sprigs (with stems)
- 6 thyme sprigs or 2 teaspoons dried, crumbled
- 2 bay leaves
- 1 tablespoon tomato paste or 2 large tomatoes, coarsely chopped
- 1 large shallot, minced
- 1 large garlic clove, minced
  Mushroom trimmings (optional)
  Chicken, beef, veal or ham trimmings and bones (optional)
- 2 tablespoons Cognac
  Salt and freshly ground pepper

Melt 2 tablespoons butter in heavy 4-quart saucepan over low heat. Add onion, carrot, celery and prosciutto. Cover and cook 15 minutes, stirring occasionally. Transfer to bowl.

Melt ½ cup butter in same saucepan over low heat. Add flour and stir until roux is the color of coffee with cream, about 10 minutes. Whisk in boiling stock. Increase heat and stir until sauce returns to boil. Add reserved onion mixture to saucepan with parsley, thyme, bay leaves, tomato paste, shallot, garlic and trimmings and bones. Reduce heat and simmer, skimming off foam that rises to surface, until sauce has thickened and is reduced to 1 quart, about 3 hours, stirring occasionally toward end of cooking time to prevent sticking. Strain sauce through chinois or sieve lined with 3 layers of dampened cheesecloth, but do not press down on ingredients or sauce will be cloudy. Remove any fat from surface of sauce by blotting with strips of paper towel. Just before serving, stir in Cognac and season to taste with salt and pepper.

Newburg Sauce

MAKES 1½ CUPS

- 1 cup Béchamel Sauce
- ¼ cup heavy cream
- 2 egg yolks, slightly beaten
  Cayenne pepper to taste
- 2 tablespoons sherry or 1 tablespoon sherry and 1 tablespoon brandy

Heat Béchamel Sauce in top of double boiler over boiling water. Stir cream into sauce. Pour in egg yolks, whisking constantly. Add pepper. Just before serving stir in sherry or sherry and brandy.

Béchamel Sauce

MAKES 1½ CUPS (MEDIUM CONSISTENCY)

- 3 tablespoons butter
- ¼ cup finely chopped onion
- 3 tablespoons all purpose flour
- 2 cups scalded milk, half and half or whipping cream
- ¼ teaspoon salt
- 3 white peppercorns
- 1 parsley sprig
- ¼ celery stalk, thinly sliced
  Pinch of nutmeg

In heavy 2-quart saucepan (do not use an aluminum pan), melt butter over low heat. Add onion and cook until soft but not browned. Whisk in flour to make roux. Cook, whisking constantly, until roux is frothy and free of lumps, about 2 to 3 minutes. Remove saucepan from heat and slowly add half the hot liquid, whisking constantly. Add remaining liquid and continue whisking until sauce is smooth, about 3 to 5 minutes. Return sauce to medium-low heat and add remaining ingredients. Simmer uncovered, stirring frequently with wooden spoon (be careful not to miss outer edges of saucepan), until sauce is reduced by about one-fourth, approximately 20 to 30 minutes. Remove saucepan from heat and strain.

176 Hollandaise Sauce

Vélouté Sauce

MAKES ABOUT 1¾ CUPS

¼ cup water*
1½ tablespoons fresh lemon juice
¼ teaspoon salt
Pinch of freshly ground white
pepper
3 egg yolks
1 cup (2 sticks) unsalted butter,
melted

Mix water, lemon juice, salt and pepper in small saucepan. Bring to a boil, reduce heat and simmer until liquid is reduced to 2 tablespoons. Set pan in a larger pan of cold water to cool.

Beat yolks in heavy, nonaluminum, 1-quart saucepan** until thick and creamy. Slowly beat in lemon reduction. Whisk over very low heat (or beat with electric mixer set on medium speed) until thickened, about 3 to 4 minutes. Do not allow eggs to become too thick or dry. Remove from heat and begin slowly drizzling warm, not hot, melted butter into yolks, beating constantly until all butter has been added and sauce is just pourable. If it is too thick to pour, thin with a little hot water.

*If serving sauce with fish, substitute white wine, dry vermouth or clam juice for water.
**If a heavy pan is not available, protect the sauce from direct heat by standing pan on a heatproof pad, or over 2 inches of very hot, but not simmering, water. If hollandaise sauce is made in a double boiler, eggs will require about 10 minutes of constant beating to reach the correct consistency.

Follow directions for making béchamel, replacing milk or cream with chicken, fish or veal stock, depending on the food the sauce is to be served with.

Piecrust

MAKES ONE 9- OR 10-INCH PASTRY
SHELL

1½ cups flour
¼ cup (½ stick) butter
¼ cup solid vegetable shortening
¼ teaspoon salt
Grated peel of 1 lemon or 1 small
orange (optional)
¼ cup cold water *or* orange or
lemon juice combined with water

Beaten egg white *or* Apricot
Glaze* (optional)

Lightly grease 9- or 10-inch pie pan. With an electric mixer, blend flour, butter, shortening, salt and peel, if desired, until mixture forms pieces the size of peas. Add liquid and mix until dough comes clean from sides of bowl and forms a ball. Flatten ball into 8-inch circle, wrap in plastic and refrigerate 30 minutes.

Transfer chilled dough to lightly floured working surface and roll into 12-inch circle, rolling from center of circle toward the outer rim.

Lightly flour rolling pin and pastry. Place rolling pin on edge of pastry circle and roll dough over

rolling pin. Gently unroll dough onto pie pan. Without forcing or stretching dough, press it into pie pan, taking care that dough is not too thick where bottom and sides meet. Allow 1 inch of dough to hang over edge of pan; trim off excess. Turn overhanging dough under to form a narrow rolled rim. Flute edge.

Preheat oven to 400°F. With fork, prick sides and bottom of shell (if recipe calls for an unbaked shell, do not prick dough). Cut piece of waxed paper to fit over dough and press firmly onto dough. Cover with layer of rice, lima beans or baker's beans to prevent shrinking; make sure they are scattered evenly. Bake 25 minutes. Remove paper and rice or beans (save for use in other pie crusts). Return pie crust to oven until lightly browned, approximately 5 minutes. Cool, paint with egg white or apricot glaze (use egg white for savory tarts and quiches, apricot glaze for dessert pies) and fill as desired.

*Apricot Glaze
1 11-ounce jar apricot preserves
¼ cup apricot brandy or Cognac

Puree preserves with brandy in blender or food processor. Store in tightly covered jar in refrigerator.

NOTE: Apricot glaze is delicious over fresh fruit.

INDEX

178

180